ESCAPING FANTASYLAND

Overcoming pornography
one decision at a time

STEVEN L. SHOWALTER

WORD AFLAME PRESS
WELDON SPRING, MO

Word Aflame Press
36 Research Park Court, Weldon Spring, MO 63304
pentecostalpublishing.com

Printed in the United States of America

Cover design by Andy Van Engen

26 25 24 23 22 21 20 19 18 17   1 2 3 4 5

Library of Congress Cataloging-in-Publication Data

Names: Showalter, Steven L., author.
Title: Escaping fantasyland : overcoming pornography one decision at a time / Steven L. Showalter.
Description: Weldon Spring, MO : Word Aflame Press, [2017] | Includes bibliographical references. |
Identifiers: LCCN 2017023327 (print) | LCCN 2017036722 (ebook) | ISBN 9780757754456 () | ISBN 9780757754449 (alk. paper)
Subjects: LCSH: Pornography--Religious aspects--Christianity. | Sex addiction--Religious aspects--Christianity.
Classification: LCC BV4597.6 (ebook) | LCC BV4597.6 .S56 2017 (print) | DDC 241/.667--dc23
LC record available at https://lccn.loc.gov/2017023327

ESCAPING FANTASYLAND

This book is dedicated to those bound by pornography and similar sexual sins. It is my prayer that you will find God's direction and strength to gain spiritual victory. I also dedicate it to my wife for standing by my side during my conflict and helping me during my struggle.

Contents

ACKNOWLEDGEMENTS

Thank you to my wife Angela, and my children Natalie and Austin, who have been very patient with me through the slow and tedious process of researching and writing this book. I love you very much.

I wish to extend a great big thank you to numerous family members and friends who have prayed for me, offered encouragement, constructive criticism, and suggestions.

Special thanks to:

Daniel J. Koren for your many recommendations, rewrites, and direction. This book most likely would not be a reality without your encouragement.

Tony J. Roberts for your assistance. Thank you for making this readable.

Kaitlyn Huffman and Shawnelle Alley for your assistance with Angela's perspective.

INTRODUCTION

But where sin abounded, grace abounded much more, so that as sin reigned in death, even so grace might reign through righteousness to eternal life through Jesus Christ our Lord (Romans 5:20–21).

Pornography plagues our society, devastating millions of men and women. Through enchantment and seduction, it has snared many people in its chains. This sinful device has trapped numerous men, but we are naive if we think only men struggle with this. Porn is drawing in women at an ever increasing and alarming pace. We see the effects this has on children as well. Many girls and boys begin sexting as early as elementary school.

Consider the scandal that rocked Canon City High School in Colorado in late 2015. Over one hundred students were involved in a sexting ring in which they traded nude photos of themselves. Between three hundred to four hundred nude photos circulated among students, including pictures of eighth graders.

This problem has silently crept into church after church. Here is a startling example that may open your eyes: In 2014, I conducted a survey of apostolic men at a men's conference. Of the men attending, 100 percent stated they had either seen pornography or been tempted by it. Sadly, this is not just a worldly issue; it is also an issue within the church. How do I know?

Let me introduce myself.

My name is Steve, and I was held captive by pornography for many years. I'm thankful God set me free from the bondage of this devastating sin. I am a preacher's kid and now a pastor myself. This book contains my story and what I have learned along the way.

Many people view porn, take drugs, drink, overeat, or commit other compulsive, sinful habits to alleviate frustration, mask pain, soothe anger, and relieve boredom, among other reasons. Sadly, these just exacerbate their problems; committing sin never solves anything. Pornography leaves behind a trail of broken and empty lives. Jesus died on Calvary to change that. He suffered so we could be free. He came to restore life to fallen humanity. However, one must make the conscious decision to turn away from sin and turn toward Jesus.

The chains of pornography and erotica bind many people, including Christians. In my opinion, it is the most common sin hidden within the church. Those who are bound want freedom, help, and hope! They are looking for answers. If you are struggling with porn or related sins, it is my prayer that this testimony gives you the directions and answers needed to help you win this fight. This book will equip you to win the war with pornography. Pornography can be defeated. I pray God revolutionizes your life and helps you become the child of God that both you and He want you to be.

MY DIRTY SECRET

He who covers his sins will not prosper, but whoever confesses and forsakes them will have mercy (Proverbs 28:13).

You have set our iniquities before You, our secret sins in the light of Your countenance (Psalm 90:8).

My heart pounded. My pulse raced. I could feel each surge of blood as it pumped through my veins. I had never felt such an intense physical thrill like that before. I was on a mission.

For weeks, I had planned for this day. The adrenaline rush overwhelmed me as I allowed my carnal lust to drive me to do something I had never done before. I entered Waldenbooks and quickly scanned the store for any familiar faces. Finding none, I headed straight for the magazine rack. This time, I was not looking to purchase *Road & Track*. I was going for something far more appealing than the latest Ferrari or Mustang GT spread. I quickly scanned the magazine covers and chose a *Penthouse*.

At age eighteen, I was about to purchase my very first pornographic magazine. I knew I would have to show my ID, but I did not care. The cashier just happened to be a woman. I felt a tiny bit sheepish placing my selection on the counter, but what could she say? I was legal.

The trip homeward turned into a blur. I slipped the magazine under my jacket and went straight to my room. I could not wait to see what these alluring women had to offer me, and they delivered what my carnal heart longed for. I felt I had arrived. I would no longer have to rely on luck to drop porn into my hands. I had the power to get what I wanted whenever I wanted.

And so it began.

Okay, it did not begin there, it just escalated significantly. This problem started when I, an innocent eight-year-old boy, was visiting my grandmother's house. A friend found his dad's stash of hidden porn magazines and showed them to me. For the first time in my life, I was staring at a naked woman. I was captivated and did not know exactly why. I knew it was wrong to look, but the model on the page seemed to be inviting me to explore every inch of her. I was not yet sexually mature, so I was not dealing with physical reactions. I knew it was naughty, but I couldn't tear my eyes away.

Even though this occurred many years ago, I can still recall that very moment. I remember the pose and how it affected me. I remember being afraid my grandma would catch us. Looking through the magazine gave me a high my young mind did not understand.

From that moment on, viewing porn was a rare opportunity, but each time it had the same breathtaking adrenaline rush and pulse-pounding reaction. Moreover, it started to affect me in other ways. With sexual maturity came new and electrifying effects—each more intense than before. One time I entered a bookstore at a mall. Pornography filled the magazine rack next to the cashier. Temptation overwhelmed this young teen, and I started looking through a magazine. I was in public and didn't care if I got caught. In fact, I did get caught—by a woman standing in line. She scolded me and I was embarrassed.

When I could not find porn, the lingerie section of a catalog became a substitute. Still, I found nothing as exciting as seeing a nude woman on the pages of a magazine—at least, not until I found something that would top that experience. When I was fourteen, I found some pornographic videos. They belonged to a man I looked up to and respected. Those videos became a chain that would bind me for years to come. Seeing men and women together doing things my fourteen-year-old eyes should not see, set me on a path that eventually led to a place of hopelessness and fear. Knowing this person had those movies caused confusion and added to my sense of hopelessness. I felt doomed.

After my initial purchase following my eighteenth birthday, I bought magazines frequently and rented adult videos when my parents were away from home. I became more and more ensnared, like an insect in a spider's web. I knew I was doing wrong; I knew it was sin; I knew I needed help. I just did not know how to free myself from the trap I was in.

Although my actions may not have shown it, my heart's desire was to live for God. I had attended church my whole life and enjoyed it. The best night of my life was the night I received the Holy Ghost, at the tender age of eleven. I loved going to youth camps and other church functions to be with my friends. But mostly I loved feeling the presence of God. Why then was I struggling with something I knew was so wrong? What was wrong with me? I felt pulled in opposite directions.

Although I tried to resist and fight the urges for porn, I surrendered to it at every opportunity. I seemed to have lost all control. Around the year 1992, I attended church camp for a week. The power of God visited the services and the preaching was anointed. I enjoyed a great move of the Holy Ghost and God's power invigorated me; it was the greatest, most amazing experience. Camp ended Friday night.

Saturday, as I drove home, that familiar urge hit me. I had gone a whole week without my fix and needed one at that moment. Instead of going straight home, I made a detour to an adult bookstore and paid for a few minutes of porn at one of the arcade booths. Afterward, it felt as though I had violated the entire week of camp for a few moments of self-indulgence.

How would I make it if I could not stay spiritually healthy any longer than that? For the next couple of years, my habit remained about the same. Church was still the most important aspect of my life, but I continued viewing porn whenever I could. I never gave up trying to live for God. Although I considered it many times, I could not bring myself to quit the church. My Holy Ghost experience was too real to leave.

In early 1994, I became engaged to my girlfriend, Angela, who is also a preacher's kid. We met when her family was stationed in Omaha in the early 1980s; her father was in the Navy. She is four years my senior and quick to remind me of the Bible verse that teaches, "Obey your elders." Please pray for me!

While engaged, I believed that the intimate relationship of marriage would solve my porn problems. I would soon have a God-endorsed sexual partner and would no longer need porn.

We married in September 1994 and settled in Nebraska. My wife was from Indiana and had no immediate family in the area. Since she had trouble finding a job right away, she made an arrangement with her former employer in Indiana that would allow her to work anytime she went home for a visit.

She made numerous trips back and forth for the next few years. My porn problem returned every time she left. She would hit the road and so would I—she to Indiana and I to the store where I rented adult videos. It proved to be a reliable way for me to get my fixes.

I hated what I did. I was ashamed to tell my new bride what I did while she was away; she would have been devastated. I was afraid that if she knew, she would not come home. This fear and the disappointment with myself struck me, and I knew I was being unfaithful.

In 1997, we moved to a home with an office on the second floor. We purchased our first computer—a Compaq desktop with a 4GB hard drive. Impressive I know. It did something amazing: it plugged into a phone line that would connect me to the World Wide Web.

This technology allowed me to surf the Internet and download all kinds of stuff. In my case, it ended up being lots of porn. When I got off work, I headed straight to the office. I would wait the agonizing five minutes to connect via dial-up. Then I had to wait while the pictures or short video clips would load. In the beginning this had been a rare occurrence; now it had become an everyday habit, sometimes several times a day.

I lived in Fantasyland.

I was so ensnared that I thought about porn almost constantly. I would sit in church and feel utterly defeated in knowing I would watch porn after getting home. Although I hated where I was and what I had become, I had no idea how to escape. I kept this aspect of my life hidden from everyone. It was my dirty secret.

In early 1998, my wife and I found out we were expecting our first child and waited with anticipation for our daughter to be born. The thought hit me that I needed to stop the pornography because I was about to become a dad. But that was all it ended up being—just a thought. I could not figure out how to quit.

I felt God calling me to the ministry, but I resisted. How could I possibly tell people that Jesus could set them free from sin when I seemed helplessly bound myself? That would be sheer hypocrisy.

I was afraid to tell anyone about my habit. If I did, I believed my wife would be gone, my new daughter would be gone, and I would lose whatever ministry I had. I would be on the street with nothing to show for my life. I just knew it would be the end of me. I was scared and desperately needed help, but I didn't know to whom to turn; I couldn't talk to just anyone about this issue. The fear of total failure plagued me. What a lonely, miserable life! I learned to pretend things were okay, but inside I was a mess.

During the many years in bondage, I felt completely alone. I was sure I was the only guy in church who struggled with this. Telling anyone about it was too embarrassing to consider. If my friends knew, what would they think or say? Could I show my face in public? I wondered why I couldn't struggle with something else, like cigarettes or alcohol. Why did it have to be pornography? I felt like a fraud—what a hypocrite! What a loser! On the outside I looked like a good, God-fearing man. On the inside, I was harboring a dark, dirty secret that I just could not overcome.

I pleaded with God, "Either help me or kill me." I even asked Him to remove all sexual desire from my life. When I prayed, I did not hear from God and thought He was ignoring me. "Is there any hope for me, God? Why can't I break free from this sin?"

God finally answered my prayers. It took time, patience, and a tremendous amount of self-examination, but by the grace of God, I broke free from the bondage of porn. Through this journey, I have learned many valuable lessons, principles, and truths. I have experienced many battles, failures, and ultimate victories. The greatest insight I gained, however, was this:

I learned that by God's grace I could be free from pornography one decision at a time.

WHY IS THIS
HAPPENING TO ME?

I cry out, " My splendor is gone! Everything I had hoped for from the LORD is lost! The thought of my suffering and homelessness is bitter beyond words" (Lamentations 3:18–19, NLT).

Growing up in a pastor's home gave me a firm grasp of right and wrong. As I have already stated, when I was eleven, I received the Holy Ghost according to the Acts 2:38 message. Yet I was hooked on porn. Having God's Spirit living within is supposed to prevent things like this, right? So why was this consuming me?

Allow me to go into a little more depth. In my early teen years, which naturally come with raging hormones, I became interested in girls. God gives us a normal sexual appetite, but in my youth, I did not know how to distinguish between the norm and my carnal desires. Satan plays off of that appetite, creating confusion. When lust takes root and grows, it perverts our thoughts and feelings. I did not want a friendship or relationship to be centered on sex, as porn suggested.

During my senior year of high school, I was in the Junior Reserve Officer Training Corps (JROTC), which required that I attend the annual Military Ball. It was also required that I take a date; I could not attend alone. The big date just happened to occur shortly after my first porn purchase.

There was a girl on my JROTC rifle team whom I enjoyed spending time with—all the guys did. She was a cute, outgoing, life-of-the-party kind of girl. She loved flirting with boys, and the guys enjoyed giving her attention. She reveled in being surrounded by all the testosterone. I decided to ask her to the ball and she accepted. I debated asking a girl from church but did not want to send the message that I was romantically interested in her.

The ball was a big deal for seniors, as it was our moment to shine. Guys had to wear their formal uniforms and girls wore formal ball gowns. I wanted us to arrive in style, so I ordered a limo. I also bought a corsage and made plans for an elegant dinner. That was the easy part. The difficult part was that I would be with this cute, flirtatious girl, facing incredible temptation. The possibility that the night could end with sex weighed on my mind for days.

I feared making an enormous mistake. I worried about the consequences of my actions: an unwanted pregnancy or committing to a relationship that would never work in the long run. Still, the idea of satisfying my desires was incredibly tempting. The battle raged in my mind. I wanted to be a man and have fun, but at the same time, I wanted to be a gentleman and treat her right. The flesh was warring against the Spirit! What to do?

I decided to purchase condoms just in case, and headed to the store. But once I got there, I was too embarrassed to buy them and just drove home. How crazy is that? I could buy pornographic material but not condoms. Ultimately, I knew crossing that line would lead me down a spiritual road I was afraid to travel. Porn was simply looking at nude pictures; acting it out would include another person in my sin.

It was as if I stood at a locked door with the key in my hand, clueless of any idea what was on the other side. I could unlock the door and face some severe consequences, or I could leave it locked. I could not put my feelings and thoughts into words at that moment, but I felt extremely cautious. "God, help me!" I prayed.

I established boundary lines and was determined not to cross them.

God did help! Finally, I made my choice. For fear of sin's consequences and out of respect for my date, I chose to leave that door locked; I *chose* not to go there. Once my decision was made, the turmoil that had plagued me left. I felt total peace with my decision and no longer feared the evening with my date. I remember thinking, *I may be the only guy she ever dates that doesn't attempt taking advantage of her, and that will leave a lasting impression on her.* Time has proven this thought to be correct.

The big night came. The limo arrived and we proceeded to her house. I walked to the door and rang the bell. When she stepped out, she was stunning. I met her parents, thinking, *Your daughter is safe with me.* We got into the limo, and I will never forget the first thing she said: "Uniforms turn me on."

There it was. The green light! But my mind was made up. I had established boundary lines and was determined not to cross them! I had chosen to be a gentleman. I did not take advantage of her, and thankfully she did not push herself on me. In fact, she was a lady, and for that I am incredibly grateful!

We are still friends to this day. While we are not close, we can talk without the awkwardness or guilt that would have come from crossing that line. We have a mutual respect between us. My wife has met her, and they talk like old friends. I have no regrets about my decision. Had I made that mistake, though, this certainly would not be the case.

I failed to make the connection that viewing pornography was also a choice.

Why did I share that? Because porn use had made my inhibitions weak and I was on the verge of going even deeper into sin. Thank God He helped me make the right choice and put a determination within me to do what was right. What I couldn't understand was my ability to say no to one sin but not the other. Why was the sin of pornography so different for me? What I failed to realize was that viewing pornography was also a choice. *Sin is always a choice!*

After graduating from high school in 1989, I submitted my application to a local college and was accepted. Something happened, however, that changed my plans. Before classes started, my buddies and I traveled to Texas to visit some mutual friends. While there, we planned to visit Texas Bible College (TBC), since one of the guys in my group planned to attend that fall. I was not interested in Bible college. Why would I be? I did not feel a call to the ministry. Besides, I certainly was not in a position to minister to someone else in view of my dirty secret.

While in Houston, we visited the TBC campus as well as Life Tabernacle, a large church pastored by James Kilgore at the time. Suddenly, God started talking to me about attending TBC. After spending time in prayer and with some definite confirmation, I submitted my application. I felt strongly that I was in the will of God. I had the misconception, though, that if I did what God wanted, He would remove the desire for pornography from my heart. I expected it to be automatic. Sadly, I was wrong.

Due to lack of self-discipline, my porn habit grew.

While on campus, I did not purchase or view porn, although the desire lurked in the shadows of my mind. I knew better than to bring magazines onto campus, so I fantasized about porn. Two years later, when I returned home, I also returned to porn; I was still bound. Due to lack of self-discipline, my porn habit grew.

I remember thinking, "What happened to the deal You made me, God? I'm still hooked on pornography." As it turned out, God had not made a deal with me. There was no such thing as "Do this for me and I will do that for You." So what in the world was I going to do now? I could not walk away from God. If I quit trying to live right, I knew I would be without hope; my life already felt hopeless. But living for God was so difficult. I was trying, but failing miserably!

I started working in the security department at a large hotel in downtown Omaha and soon received a managerial promotion. I enjoyed the work, responsibility, and the trust placed in me. Unfortunately, I learned how to access the hotel porn movies. When things were calm, I could go to the control room and watch whatever porn video was showing. Viewing porn was not what I was entrusted to do, and that certainly did not help me overcome it.

It was during this time that I married. Working at the hotel was stressful, and the hours were long. I wanted to be home with my wife in the evenings, so I stepped down from my management position, planning to go back to college to get my teaching degree. Once again, God had other plans.

I began working at the US Postal Service as a letter carrier. God gave me a better job with evenings off. I was even able to attend church on Sundays. But this job did nothing to rid me of my daily porn habit. No, this new career came with many dangers, and I am not talking about dogs! There was an incessant barrage of lingerie catalogs and magazine articles on sex. Almost weekly Victoria's Secret mailed a new catalog. (Thankfully, this is no longer their practice.)

Why couldn't I break free?

Pornography. It had a firm, cruel grip on my life, and I could not figure out a plan of escape. I felt like Jacob Marley in *A Christmas Carol*, wrapped in chains and padlocks. In the play, Jacob came back to warn Ebenezer Scrooge he was making the same mistakes in life that he himself had made. Unfortunately for Marley, it was too late to change anything; he was dead. I, however, was not, and I needed my chains and padlocks removed. I wondered if I was doomed to live like this forever. Why couldn't I break free?

I was weary from fighting against this bondage of pornography and convinced that something was wrong with me. I cried out to God for help, but He seemed so far away! I wasn't even sure He still cared about me after all the things I had done. I was trying to live for Him but it seemed He was doing nothing to help me. I was frustrated, desperate, and felt so lost! I wanted to experience real joy, God's peace and love, and true freedom.

I was a preacher's kid. I attended Bible college. I felt called to the ministry. Pornography was a dirty sin that sinners battle. So why was this happening to me?

3

LEARNING TO FIGHT

Be sober, be vigilant; because your adversary the devil walks about like a roaring lion, seeking whom he may devour (I Peter 5:8).

The year was 1999. A guest minister at our church asked to speak privately with my wife and me. I did not find this unusual as we were aspiring to the ministry and assumed he would share words of encouragement with us. The talk, however, was different than anticipated. Sitting together, he began to share knowledge of a struggle that affects many families today, including those in the ministry. He then spoke one word, which struck tremendous fear in my heart—*pornography*. Uh-oh, I thought, *this is not going to be good.*

The moment I had feared for so many years had finally arrived. Although I had not said a word to this man about my sin, he knew. I recognized the fact that I needed to talk to someone about this, but not in front of my wife! I wasn't sure what to do. If I didn't confess, she would know I was covering up something. If I did, it was not going to be pretty. I felt I was in a lose-lose situation. Put on the spot, there was no hiding the issue any longer.

I wanted help from the Lord, but this is not what I had in mind. I was about to reveal my darkest, dirtiest secret. Finally, with encouragement from the minister, I opened up to my wife and discussed the struggle that had stalked me for so long.

After my confession, all the emotions and thoughts I had feared came boiling to the surface. It felt like my soul had been ripped open and stripped bare. Certainly, my dignity and self-respect were gone. I was nothing more than a rotten sinner who desperately needed help. I longed for support but believed all the fears that had haunted me would come to pass: as soon as we got home my wife would pack up and leave, and I would see my daughter only on weekend visits (my son was not yet born). I felt so much shame. I felt I was by far the worst sinner in the world. The apostle Paul referred to himself as the chief of sinners, but I was right up there with him.

The drive home held mixed emotions for me; I felt awful and good at the same time. I was afraid of what would happen next, but the good I felt could be summed up in one word—relief! I knew an emotional locomotive had just hit my wife and wondered what was going through her mind. While I was feeling tremendous relief at having that heavy weight lifted, I knew she was deeply hurt. Her perception of me must have been crushed. It was like I had just admitted to committing adultery during our entire four-and-a-half years of marriage. She did not want to talk.

My confession did not fix the problem. Porn still had me bound.

Thankfully, Angela did not leave. She stated that she had made a vow to God the day we married and meant every word of it. Hearing her say this, however, did not ease my fears. The next several weeks and months were very unpleasant in the Showalter home. Even though I had acknowledged my problem with porn, my confession did not fix the problem. I still struggled;

porn still had me bound. I needed to learn how to fight against and overcome my desire for porn, but how?

Never before had I heard anyone admit to struggling with porn to the extent that I did, certainly not those in the ministry. A couple of friends mentioned they had seen porn and even struggled with it a little. I tried to find resources that addressed this subject, but only a few were available, which I found frustrating.

I had heard preachers warn against the dangers of pornography: Porn is a problem, a worldly issue, a sinful addiction, and something to be avoided. Really? Duh! These statements were obvious to me; I was living it. I already knew porn was dangerous. Knowing that porn was sinful was not enough; it did not help me overcome it. Where were the messages that taught how to be delivered from porn? Where were the words of hope? I needed real direction, not just generalized comments.

I heard about the book *Every Man's Battle*, and began reading it. For the first time in my life, I discovered something almost as important as Columbus discovering America! I learned that other men struggled with pornography, just as I did. I saw myself in many of their stories and could relate. I was not the only man who faced this; I was not alone in the world! In fact, many men struggle with porn, albeit silently and alone. Unfortunately, this also includes Christian men. Finally, I had a resource that got me headed in the right direction. I learned of many valuable principles and tools to utilize in this fight against pornography and am forever grateful for the book.

I am a Christian man who has experienced the new birth through repentance, baptism in Jesus' name, and the infilling of the Holy Ghost just like the early church in the Book of Acts. By definition, I am saved from a life of sin. How could I still be living in sin? It baffled me. I had had the doctrinal truth of the salvation message instilled in me since childhood. I was settled on that fact, but I was having extreme difficulty reconciling the new birth and my sorry, sinful self. What was my problem? Why did it seem my salvation experience was not saving me from my sin?

I knew how to repent, or so I thought. Repentance is asking God to forgive you of your sins and turning your back on sin. I had done this so many times that it had become almost ritualistic. I would look at porn while knowing it was wrong, and then repent. I wondered how God could forgive me of the sin I had just finished committing—especially when He knew I would end up repeating the same sin the very next day. Repentance just never seemed to work, that is, until I figured out why: I had failed to recognize my role in repentance. True repentance is not just asking for forgiveness; it is making a conscious choice and effort to turn away from sin.

I had to learn to forgive myself and stop wallowing in the mud.

God's grace is sufficient (II Corinthians 12:9). That is what His Word says. His Word also says if we confess our sins, He is faithful and just to forgive us and cleanse us from wrongdoing (I John 1:9). If God had forgiven me, from where was this feeling of condemnation coming? Why didn't I feel forgiven, and why did porn still have such a strong grip on me? The answer is, freedom doesn't just happen automatically when we ask God to forgive us. We must take an active role by learning godly principles and living them. It was then I realized that, although God had forgiven me, I had to learn to forgive myself and stop wallowing in the mud. I had to quit holding my past failures over my own head. True repentance involves exercising self-control and living forgiven.

The pleasure and excitement a man derives from seeing a nude woman is natural but inappropriate outside of the guidelines God has provided. It is our responsibility to line up to His teachings by exercising self-control. That is what I lacked. I had absolutely no spiritual discipline when it came to pornography. I had mistakenly thought the Holy Ghost was supposed make me do right, but I had thought wrong. I had to learn to control myself.

God's Spirit will work in our lives only when we allow Him to—when we surrender completely like clay on a potter's wheel. God will not force us to do anything against our will. If a person wants to look at porn, the Holy Ghost will warn them, but He will not stop them. He will provide a way to escape, but taking the escape route is ultimately our own decision. If we do not place our will in God's hands, we will succumb to the desires of our flesh.

When faced with temptation, we decide to either follow our carnal nature or we choose to do what is best for us and follow God's Word.

We are not puppets being manipulated by a Holy Ghost ventriloquist. The Holy Ghost is not a mind-control agent. God's Spirit gives us the power to overcome sin and our carnal desires; it changes the desires in our heart. The Holy Ghost will teach us, guide us, and give us spiritual power, but we must use the Holy Ghost correctly. When faced with temptation, we decide to either follow our carnal nature or we choose to do what is best for us and follow God's Word. The Holy Ghost prompts us to do what is right and will give guidance on how to accomplish that. The Holy Ghost will guide us into all truth (John 16:13).

Little by little, I started putting into practice what I was learning. Slowly I began to make progress. It was a challenging and painful process that took a few years. I wish it would have happened quicker, but I had much to learn and very few resources to guide me.

As I began my journey toward freedom, I started researching pornography in a different way. I felt an overwhelming desire to understand the industry. I wanted to know the truth behind the façade. Why do we never hear the negative side of this "delightful" fantasyland like sexually transmitted diseases (STDs), abuse, drugs, alcohol, and much more? What is this deceptive industry hiding? I saved every news story, article, research paper, and statistic I could find. I did the same with every story I found concerning those who escaped the grip of pornography. I collected all this information onto my computer and began printing out items, saving them into a binder. After going through a ream of paper and who knows how many ink cartridges, I stopped printing anything new.

On occasion, I would still stumble and watch porn, but this time, it was different. When I fell, I would stop and mentally rewind the hours and days in my mind to the last time I slipped up. This allowed me to see if I had omitted anything such as prayer or studying the Word of God.

I began to see a pattern develop and recognized some triggers that caused temptation: boredom, frustration, and physical things like a cute female jogger. One big fad occurring at that time was shorts intentionally designed to draw attention to the female anatomy. Words written across the seat of the shorts indicated if she played volleyball or soccer or participated in some other activity.

Thankfully, these shorts are no longer a fad. Unfortunately, they have been replaced with yoga pants and leggings, which are merely thin pieces of material stretched skintight. In addition, there are inappropriately low necklines, and most men I know will stare at what this reveals. The world's philosophy is, "If you've got it, flaunt it."

Our carnal nature wants to do a double take. We glance in the rearview mirror. We turn to see her after she has passed us. We circle the area for another look. We walk by the Victoria's Secret store instead of the other side of the mall just to see the huge posters.

I heard the story of a two-year-old boy walking through a mall with his parents. They passed a Victoria's Secret display, and the two-year-old's eyes were so fixed on the model that he slammed into a support pillar. Even at that young age, the female form had a captivating effect on him.

I averted my eyes from the danger zone and quoted Scripture.

Instead of gawking, I learned the art of averting my eyes while quoting Scripture—two different lines of attack in one maneuver. That is, I tried to. It did not work too well at first because for too long I had allowed my eyes to feast on female delicacies. I could not remember key Bible verses, so I typed up a cheat sheet and placed it in my wallet. In time of need I took it out, read a few verses, and prayed, "God, let me see women as souls just as You do instead of being tempted by their bodies."

It took practice, but I noticed it was beginning to work. I could drive along, see a jogger ahead of me, start quoting Scripture, and look somewhere else. My wife also played a crucial role in my deliverance. If she saw something she thought might cause me to mentally stumble, she would distract my attention. I learned to trust her. If she said, "Don't look over there," I looked elsewhere. She was protecting me.

Every phase of this journey felt like detox. I was unlearning bad habits and replacing them with new, healthy habits. I was getting stronger, but I was not free yet. I was still bound and still frustrated by that fact. Why? I had done everything I learned from the available resources. I was accountable, used Scripture when tempted, averted my eyes, and had an Internet filter.

At that point, I realized there was more to this journey than what a Christian resource guide could teach. While living for God, real freedom will occur only one way: by living totally submitted to Jesus Christ through the new birth experience. God's desire is for us to be completely and totally free. He does not want to partially deliver us because that would not be freedom at all.

I had about fifteen or twenty secular CDs I had purchased over the years. They were not acid rock or anything extreme—not wicked by definition—but God started talking to me about throwing them out. I put them in a bag with the intention of tossing them in the trash, but found myself putting it off. God would remind me from time to time that He wanted me to have a deeper relationship with Him, and I needed to let go of the CDs. I should have obeyed Him, but instead I put them on the back burner with the intention of getting rid of them later.

My wife went on another trip out of town. I had been doing very well in overcoming my porn habit, but I wasn't free yet. Sure enough, when she left, I took off to buy porn. Caving in to my carnal desires was extremely frustrating, and I decided to have a serious discussion with God about my lack of progress. I had a good prayer meeting but still no breakthrough. God reminded me about the CDs, and I asked, "God, what does that bag of CDs have to do with my porn habit?"

It had been well over a year since He started talking to me about the CDs, and I decided I had delayed throwing them out long enough. Out of frustration I opened each one and busted it into little pieces. As I did, I literally felt the fingers of pornography begin to lift off of me. When the last CD broke, I was free from porn, and I knew it! I had never felt so free in all my life. That is when it hit me: God wants us to have complete freedom. What good is it to set me free from porn when I willfully disobey Him and am bound by sin in other areas? God does not want to just set us free from the sins we do not like; He wants us to be totally free from all besetting sins.

> Therefore we also, since we are surrounded by so great a cloud of witnesses, let us lay aside every weight, and the sin which so easily ensnares us, and let us run with endurance the race that is set before us (Hebrews 12:1).

My CDs were spiritual weights that distracted me and slowed me down. God had told me I needed to remove them from my life because they were not good for me. The sin occurred when God said to get rid of them but I disobeyed. Disobedience is a sin.

King Saul had this problem when God instructed him to kill the Amalekites in I Samuel 15. God told him to destroy every living creature, man, woman, boy, and girl. Instead, Saul spared the king and the best of the sheep and oxen to sacrifice. He completely disregarded God's instructions and then insisted he had done what God told him to do. Samuel made this statement that still rings true today: "Has the LORD as great delight in burnt offerings and sacrifices, as in obeying the voice of the LORD? Behold, to obey is better than sacrifice, and to heed than the fat of rams" (I Samuel 15:22). It is interesting to note that an Amalekite was present at Saul's death. What we refuse to kill ultimately has the potential to destroy us.

Being tempted is inevitable; contending with it is a choice.

My freedom from the enemy's chains will not be entirely complete until my days on earth are over. While I am no longer bound, my fight is ongoing. Temptation will always be there, but I don't have to give in. I can choose to contend with it. I told my wife, "I may lose a battle, but I will not lose this war." That is not an excuse to slip up, but it is my declaration of ultimate victory. Thankfully, by putting these methods, tools, and protections in place, I know how to win when temptations arise. The fight is much easier now because I know how to fight. Furthermore, I do not want to lose momentum.

In the end I want to be able to say with Paul, "I have fought the good fight, I have finished the race, I have kept the faith. Finally, there is laid up for me the crown of righteousness, which the Lord, the righteous Judge, will give to me on that Day, and not to me only but also to all who have loved His appearing" (II Timothy 4:7–8).

4

SURVIVING THE NIGHTMARE
(ANGELA'S POINT OF VIEW)

A wife of noble character who can find? She is worth far more than rubies. Her husband has full confidence in her and lacks nothing of value. She brings him good, not harm, all the days of her life (Proverbs 31:10–12, NIV).

I stood at the altar on my wedding day promising to love, cherish, and obey. Steve stood next to me, the man who would become my spiritual leader and the head of my home. I had wonderful expectations of our life together and knew we were destined to have a great marriage. We were both living for God and striving to follow Him. Our relationship was founded on friendship, and we talked about everything; there were no secrets, or so I thought. Four years into our marriage, I discovered my husband was having an affair with pornography. I felt betrayed.

The knowledge of his struggle created a flood of emotional struggles for me. I remember the heavy weight that knowledge brought with it. Fear overwhelmed me; fear that someone would find out. I was sick to my stomach and even questioned if I had married the wrong man. I wondered if my family would be lost because our spiritual leader was *not* a spiritual leader at all. And I vividly recall being mad at God; mad at Him for putting me in this position.

I prayed for God's direction before I married Steve and felt total peace—my interpretation of His stamp of approval. My prayer was that God would give me a *Joseph,* one full of integrity who would do right even when no one was looking (Genesis 39:7–9). Instead, God gave me an *Achan* who sinned and tried to hide it. Achan disobeyed God by taking plunder from the enemy and hiding it under his tent. Many innocent people died because of Achan's sin (Joshua 7:21). Would my family become a casualty of Steve's sin? I cannot describe the battle that raged in my mind, and words cannot express the grief I felt. I did not know what to do; I even considered leaving the church.

When Steve's struggle first came to light, I prayed often for his deliverance from pornography. While at church, I pretended all was well, but in truth, a cloud of doom continually surrounded me. Our children would play at my feet, laughing, while I carried this heavy weight of knowledge that my husband was bound by some twisted desire he could not seem to shake, and I felt no joy. I prayed and then prayed more. Surely God did not expect me to remain in this marriage. I tried to follow the Golden Rule: "Do unto others . . ." I worked hard on my conduct toward Steve, trying to treat him the way I should instead of the way I wanted. Many days I did not try at all. More than once, my anger got the better of me, and I swore at him. Our relationship was like a roller coaster with many ups and downs. I hated being in this marriage.

Overcoming those emotional struggles took several years, but eventually I came to this conclusion: if it was God's will for me to marry Steve, despite being unaware of his pornography addiction, then it was also God's will for me to stay married to him, even when I found out about it. I would like to interject here that although Steve was bound by pornography, he did *not* seek a physical relationship outside our marriage. If your situation is different and your spouse has stepped out on you by physically committing adultery, please seek God's direction for counseling from either your pastor or a marriage counselor.

In Genesis 2:22, God made for Adam a helpmeet whose name was Eve. The word helpmeet simply means *one who helps.* In the story of Queen Esther, the Jews were in danger of being destroyed. They were cornered, with their backs against the wall. But before this problem had developed, God set a plan in motion to fix it. He positioned a young Jewish girl in the king's palace. Her uncle, Mordecai, said to her, "Who knows whether you have come to the kingdom for such a time as this?" (Esther 4:14). Esther fulfilled her role, the evil plot was exposed, and the Jews were saved. God always has a plan. Just as God had made Eve to be a helper for Adam and placed Esther in the palace to save the Jews, could it be that God had put me together with Steve to help him fight this battle?

Steve knew the detrimental effects of pornography on our marriage and on his spiritual walk with God. He had expressed a desire to be free of the invisible chains that bound him. He did not need me preaching to him—although some days I could have done just that! Did my role as helpmeet mean I couldn't voice my concerns? No. Communication is vital for a healthy relationship, and I needed to convey to him the worries on my mind without verbally tearing him down. He needed to know that my wedding vow was good and, despite how I was feeling inside, I wasn't going to walk out the door each time he messed up.

I know this may sound dramatic to some, but if your spouse is bringing pornography into your home, only you know the burden and heavy weights that porn brings with it. For this reason, I share my story. I also offer the following directions to you. They helped me overcome the spiritual turmoil I faced while Steve was fighting to win this war.

Be one who helps!

1. Pray for your spouse.

Don't underestimate the power of prayer. God is not dead. He still hears, and He still answers. While you're praying, ask God to show you how to help your husband and then listen for His voice. God still speaks to His people, but sometimes we are so busy we don't hear Him.

2. Do not dwell on negative thoughts.

They will come, but when they do, redirect your thoughts: Listen to anointed music and anointed preaching. Crank up the music so loud your neighbors complain! Bombard your home with preaching that talks about God's promises—promises of deliverance. It is much harder for negative thoughts to take root and grow when we are being reminded of God's ability to deliver us from anything we face!

Pray! Pray until God lifts that heaviness from you and replaces it with peace. When that heaviness threatens to return and overwhelm you, pray again! Remember we have a direct line to a God who hears.

Memorize and quote Scripture. You may want to memorize verses with your spouse.

"Do not be anxious about anything, but in everything, by prayer and petition, with thanksgiving, present your requests to God. And the peace of God, which transcends all understanding, will guard your hearts and your minds in Christ Jesus" (Philippians 4:6–7).

"I can do all things through Christ who strengthens me" (Philippians 4:13).

"Casting down imaginations, and every high thing that exalteth itself against the knowledge of God, and bringing into captivity every thought to the obedience of Christ" (II Corinthians 10:5, KJV).[1]

"Yea, though I walk through the valley of the shadow of . . ." (Psalm 23:4). Uh-oh wait, not that one! Make sure your Scripture verses apply to your situation.

"Rejoice not against me, O mine enemy: when I fall, I shall arise; when I sit in darkness, the LORD shall be a light unto me" (Micah 7:8, KJV).

"You will keep him in perfect peace, whose mind is stayed on You, because he trusts in You" (Isaiah 26:3).

God's Word *will* drive away negative thoughts! I have Bible verses written on 3" x 5" cards, which I keep with me most of the time. I pull them out and read through them anytime I need a reminder of the words of hope written on each card.

3. Don't buy in to the lies of the enemy.

It is so easy to think, *if he loved me more he would not watch pornography.* But understand, the driving desire for porn is not based on love. The sole purpose of viewing it is to satisfy the lust of the flesh. Therefore, lusting after pornography does not equal not loving one's spouse. Lust is not a synonym for love.

4. Refrain from prying.

Without a doubt, we have a right to know if our guy is being unfaithful. However, if our spouse has an accountability partner to whom he is answering, I believe it is healthier for a wife's mental well-being to know that progress is being made. Since we are fighting a mental battle ourselves, keeping a record of his failures can undermine our inner peace as well as confidence that our spouse can overcome through God. They *can* do it!

For example: When I thought my husband was gaining victory over his struggle, each time I discovered that he cheated, fell, messed up, watched pornography—whatever you want to call it—it was like someone pulled the rug out from under my feet, spiritually speaking. Overwhelming fear would return and I could hear its menacing voice say, "Steve will never win this war." This is one reason we recommend a spouse not play the role of accountability partner. (See chapter 10.)

5. Resist the urge to tattle!

Keep his struggle with pornography in confidence. If you need to talk to someone, choose a person who knows how to keep a secret. Don't throw your husband under the bus and tell everyone; use caution!

I ran into an old friend a few years back. She was getting married for the second time. I was informed that her first husband, a preacher's son, was addicted to pornography. She told her mom, and her mother encouraged her to divorce, which she did. Moms always have our best interests at heart, right? They probably do, but sometimes when it comes to their kids, a mom's unbiased thinking can go right out the window. The point I want to make is that family members *may* have a harder time being objective, so seek God's direction for someone in whom to confide.

Consider what Solomon said: "He who covers over an offense promotes love, but whoever repeats the matter separates close friends" (Proverbs 17:9 NIV).

For me, I did not breathe a word of my husband's struggle to anyone, not because of integrity on my part, but because I was simply too embarrassed to let the secret out! Had I talked with someone trustworthy, I believe it would have been helpful to share the mental burden I was carrying.

6. Communicate.

A healthy relationship requires communication. Express your concerns and be specific about how you want your spouse to help you. For example, you may ask the accountability partner to give occasional assurance that progress is being made. In turn, you can discuss with your spouse the pitfalls he faces and ways to help him get over them. I will never forget a surprising request Steve made of me. He asked that I throw away the lingerie ads from the newspaper. Seriously? Yes. It was an easy thing to do and a real eye-opener about how men are affected by the way women dress. Maintaining clear communication is vital.

7. Be proactive.

Ladies, dress in a manner that will not tempt another woman's man to fall!

At one time in my life, I wasn't sure if dressing modestly was still applicable to God's bride. Now it's a no-brainer! Just ask any man who is trying to keep his thoughts clean if it matters what we wear.

While in the midst of the battle, I wish I could say that I played my helpmeet role well but, if truth be told, I did not. Many times I wanted to leave my husband. I grumbled and complained to God about the spouse He gave me and carried bitterness in my heart against Steve, even after his chains of pornography were broken. Although Steve was over it, I was not. I wasn't over the fear that he might return to porn, or the past years of agony that I went through because of his decisions. I couldn't let go of the belief that I had worked outside of our home to financially support his addiction, instead of fulfilling my heart's desire to be a stay-at-home mom. One day I reminded him, "You put me through hell." Truly, bitterness had taken up residence where love should have been. I continued to pray.

It was in a Sunday night service that a minister preached, "Forgiveness Looses Bitterness." That message was just for me. It took awhile, but through God's mercy, I forgave my husband, and when I forgave, the bitterness left. Whether the vice you are fighting against is pornography or un-forgiveness, one thing is sure: either one will negatively impact your marriage and your spiritual walk with God.

Many of these memories have been long forgotten and no longer torment me as they once did; God has healed me of so much. I can testify that the spiritual mountain you face can be conquered. I encourage you to continue fighting to make your marriage work. Don't give up on your spouse. God can do anything when we completely surrender to Him. Pick up your tools and fight; fight as though your spiritual survival depends on it, because it does. It will be worth everything when we stand face to face with the One who set us free.

PORNICATION

For all that is in the world—the lust of the flesh, and the lust of the eyes, and the pride of life—is not of the Father but is of the world (I John 2:16).

Flee sexual immorality. Every sin that a man does is outside the body, but he who commits sexual immorality sins against his own body (I Corinthians 6:18).

B efore we continue, I must cover some technical stuff. I will attempt to do so in a way that makes it interesting and opens your understanding. For us to comprehend the problem with pornography, we need to define some terms. First, the word *pornography* is not in the Bible, so how do we know it is wrong? Through examining terms, definitions, biblical principles, and teachings, we will discover the answers.

Pornography is defined as "1: the depiction of erotic behavior (as in pictures or writing) intended to cause sexual excitement; 2: material (as books or photographs) that depicts erotic behavior and is intended to cause sexual excitement."[1]

The word *pornography* originates from two Greek words, *porne*, meaning a harlot or prostitute, and *graphein*, meaning a writing or depiction. When combined we get the literal definition "writing about prostitutes."[2]

Thus while we will not find the term pornography in the Bible, we will find the words harlot, whore, and fornication. In the New Testament these words come from the Greek word *porne*.

The Bible warns us against fornication, defined as "consensual sexual intercourse between two persons not married to each other."[3] When defined biblically, *fornication* means sexual immorality—*any* sexual activity between unmarried partners. *Thayer's Greek Definitions* includes the meanings "adultery, fornication, homosexuality, lesbianism, intercourse with animals, etc."[4]

Fornication and pornography come from the same root word.

In the New Testament, every time we see the word *fornication* or the term *sexual immorality*, it comes from the Greek word *porneia* or a derivative.[5] Does *porneia* look familiar? *Porne* and *porneia*—fornication and pornography—come from the same root word.[6] The Bible is very clear that fornication (*porneia*) is sinful. It is safe to say that pornography depicts acts of fornication. If fornication is called sin, it stands to reason that depictions of fornication would also be a sin. This fact is not open to debate.

Consider this simple mathematical equation:

If a = b and b = c, then a = c.

a – Pornography

b – Fornication

c – Sin

For the sake of argument, what about a magazine that shows nudity but no sexual acts? Is that fornication? By strict definition, yes. How so? Let me explain the nuts and bolts of the adult entertainment/pornography industry.

First, we must define *prostitution* as "the act or practice of engaging in promiscuous sexual relations, especially for money."[7]

Pornography is nothing more than legalized prostitution.

In pornography, men and women get paid to pose naked and have sex for a magazine, video, or website. A person will buy this product and get sexual gratification from it. Those posing or performing are fulfilling the role of a prostitute. The magazine, video, or website producer acts as the pimp. The purchaser/user is the john. Pornography is nothing more than legalized prostitution.

One porn star said, "What is the difference between being a porn star and being a prostitute? Fundamentally, nothing. As a porn star, you sell sex for money the same you do as a prostitute."[8]

What about a lingerie catalog or advertisement? They do not depict acts of fornication. Is it considered pornography? By strict definition, no. However, let us think about this a bit. If we are looking at and using a lingerie catalog for sexual arousal, then consider the following verses of Scripture that teach an important principle Jesus taught:

> You have heard that it was said to those of old, "You shall not commit adultery." But I say to you that whoever looks at a woman to lust for her has already committed adultery with her in his heart (Matthew 5:27–28).

If we look at a woman and lust after her, we have committed adultery with her already. Jesus did not say looking at a woman was a sin; He said looking at her and lusting for her is a sin. It is committing adultery. Lust is when we undress a woman with our eyes and sexually desire her. Merely thinking she is attractive is not lust, unless our thoughts become sexual in nature. A friend of mine involved in pornography said, "I would justify looking at women who were modest according to worldly standards, but lust is lust no matter how much clothing the object of your lust has on."

Is it possible to look at a lingerie catalog and not lust? Sure, but I do not recommend perusing one—it is not safe. It is far too easy to let our eyes and mind wander and to conceive lust. Also, we might be tempted to lock those images away in our brains and recall them later for fantasy purposes. A lingerie catalog is not any safer than going to a public beach or pool.

> For all that is in the world—the lust of the flesh,
> and the lust of the eyes, and the pride of life—is
> not of the Father but is of the world (I John 2:16).

Lust is the key to all of this. We can see how quickly lust becomes sin just by reading what happened to Eve in the Garden of Eden.

> So when the woman saw that the tree was good
> for food, that it was pleasant to the eyes, and a
> tree desirable to make one wise, she took of its
> fruit and ate. She also gave to her husband with
> her, and he ate (Genesis 3:6).

Eve saw the tree was good for food—lust of the flesh. It was pleasant to the eyes—lust of the eyes. It was a tree to be desired to make one wise—pride of life. God said not to eat of the tree. That was His only instruction. But Eve lusted for the food because it looked good and would make her wise. She disobeyed the command of God and ate of the fruit.

> But each one is tempted when he is drawn away
> by his own desires and enticed. Then, when desire
> has conceived, it gives birth to sin; and sin, when it
> is full-grown, brings forth death (James 1:14–15).

The first thing a good salesperson does is make us see our need for their product or they play off of human nature's desire to get something easy, fast, and enjoyable. The serpent was the perfect snake-oil salesman. He made the fruit appear irresistible. Why would Eve not want to try it? It was sold with the idea she could have everything she desired.

The porn industry understands the human desire for sex, so they market it in a very enticing package. You can have sex with anyone you want, anytime, anywhere. Just open your computer browser or mobile device and enjoy. It is so convenient.

Sinful lust causes us to crave what we should not have.

We all have carnal cravings. Sinful lust causes us to crave what we should not have. When something tempts us in this area, we must fight against it or we will succumb to it. That is when personal responsibility or choice comes into play. If we give in to the lust, sin is then committed. Sin results in death.

In most cases, sin involves physical action—murder, stealing, lying, and cheating. As mentioned earlier, adultery can be committed in the heart without any physical deed. If we undress a person with our eyes or view someone as an object of sexual pleasure, Jesus said we have sinned. In other words, we can create mental pornography in our minds, which is a sin.

During one science class in high school, a cheerleader sat next to me. Lucky me! Every Friday she wore her cheerleading uniform, and every Friday it was difficult to refrain from looking up her short, short skirt. I would take that mental image and store it for later. I didn't realize I was committing fornication with her even though I was not physically or even emotionally involved with her. That certainly was not the kind of chemistry I was supposed to be learning in class.

Think of those sexually charged novels sold to women by the millions. They contain no nude pictures, but, for example, the *Fifty Shades* trilogy has been dubbed "mommy porn" for a reason. While this series is relatively new, this pornographic issue for women is not. Harlequin novels have been around for many years. Women's magazines such as *Cosmopolitan, Women's Health, Redbook,* and *Glamour* are filled with sexual material. Maybe we read books or watch things that are not graphic. If their purpose is to cause sexual desire within us, we are giving in to that same lust. By definition, this is pornography: writings, pictures, and similar material intended primarily to arouse sexual desire. Pornography does not require pictures or video. Words can be pornographic.

Victoria Hearst, the granddaughter of the founder of *Cosmopolitan* magazine, said of *Cosmopolitan,* "Just label it as an adult magazine and don't sell it to kids." She continued, "The cover models are always young. It's clearly aimed at younger girls. In addition to health and beauty, they add sex positions, very graphic sexual questions and answers."[9] This magazine certainly fits the definition of pornography.

Women can lust sexually for a man just as easily as a man can for a woman.

A societal joke suggests women can drool over a buff guy and get away with it while men are called into question for checking out a cute girl. The truth is, women can lust sexually for a man just as easily as a man can for a woman. None of us, girls or guys, should be committing mental adultery with anyone.

We are sexual beings, and we all face sexual temptation to some degree in our lives. Can we please admit this fact? Whether we succumb to the temptation or defeat it will depend on us, and will be determined by how healthy our spiritual relationship is with Jesus.

What does the Bible say?

Some verses of Scripture use the terms "fornication" or "sexual immorality." Here are some examples:

> But that we write to them to abstain from things polluted by idols, from sexual immorality (Acts 15:20).

We need to abstain or not participate in sexual immorality. We must avoid or refuse to use pornography in any manner. This is a choice we must make. The responsibility falls on us.

> Do you not know that the unrighteous will not inherit the kingdom of God? Do not be deceived. Neither fornicators, nor idolaters, nor adulterers, nor homosexuals, nor sodomites, nor thieves, nor covetous, nor drunkards, nor revilers, nor extortioners will inherit the kingdom of God (I Corinthians 6:9–10).

Those that commit fornication will not make it into Heaven. Thank God for a way to be free from sin and for the opportunity to have sins forgiven!

> Flee sexual immorality. Every sin that a man does is outside the body, but he who commits sexual immorality sins against his own body (I Corinthians 6:18).

Joseph is an excellent example of someone who fled from sexual temptation (Genesis 39:7–12). The temptation he faced was not just a one-time enticement. Potiphar's wife attempted to seduce Joseph day after day, yet Joseph had the self-discipline to resist. Ultimately she grabbed him by his outer garment and he fled outdoors, leaving the garment in her hand.

> I say then: Walk in the Spirit, and you shall not fulfill the lust of the flesh. For the flesh lusts against the Spirit, and the Spirit against the flesh; and these are contrary to one another, so that you do not do the things that you wish. But if you are led by the Spirit, you are not under the law. Now the works of the flesh are evident, which are: adultery, fornication, uncleanness, lewdness . . . and the like; of which I tell you beforehand, just as I also told you in time past, that those who practice such things will not inherit the kingdom of God (Galatians 5:16–21).

Fornication is listed as one of the works of the flesh. In other words, our flesh will naturally gravitate toward these things. They are sinful, and those who commit them will not inherit Heaven. However, there is hope! If we walk in the Spirit, we will not fulfill the sinful desires of the flesh. In other words, if we do the right things, by contrast, we will not do the wrong things.

> But fornication and all uncleanness or covetousness, let it not even be named among you, as is fitting for saints; neither filthiness, nor foolish talking, nor coarse jesting, which are not fitting, but rather giving of thanks (Ephesians 5:3–4).

The saints of God should not commit fornication.

> For this is the will of God, your sanctification:
> that you should abstain from sexual immorality
> (I Thessalonians 4:3).

We are again told to abstain from fornication or *porneia*.

We cannot control everything we face in the world, but we can control what we allow into our lives.

The Bible is very clear on God's view of fornication; it is a sinful activity that must be avoided. If we are to abstain, flee from, and not let fornication be named among us, how can we invite it into our lives in the form of pornography? We cannot control everything we face in the world, but we can control what we allow into our lives. We must refrain from allowing anything that plants sexual imagery in our minds.

Solomon warned against an immoral woman in Proverbs 6. In this discourse, he wrote, "Can a man take fire to his bosom, and his clothes not be burned? Can one walk on hot coals, and his feet not be seared?" (Proverbs 6:27–28). If we play with fire, we will get burned. I have a scar on my thumb that came from playing with matches when I was a child, which proves this wise old saying. We cannot flirt with pornography and not get burned. It will add wounds and scars to our lives. Put it down and leave it behind. Abstain from it. Run from it. Flee from it. Do not go near it. It is easier said than done, but it *can* be done.

We are to guard our eyes. That does not mean just to guard against blatantly explicit material, but also subtle things—the things we read, listen to, and watch. We must avoid allowing anything into our lives that can cause sexually-explicit mental images.

Pornography presents itself in many ways. While I struggled with visual porn, others struggle with mental porn or images and thoughts they create in their own minds. Many stimuli could prompt this—real porn, sexually suggestive reading material, lust-inducing music, TV programs, or any other worldly form of entertainment. Magazines are marketed to teach young girls how to be sexy and how to be more desirable to boys. The conflict is not just a male conflict. The truth is, this is a human conflict!

WHY IS PORNOGRAPHY SO ENTICING?

The lamp of the body is the eye. If therefore your eye is good, your whole body will be full of light. But if your eye is bad, your whole body will be full of darkness. If therefore the light that is in you is darkness, how great is that darkness! (Matthew 6:22–23).

But I say to you that whoever looks at a woman to lust for her has already committed adultery with her in his heart (Matthew 5:28).

Why is pornography so enticing? Remember; its definition is "writings or pictures intended to arouse." This question is perhaps one of the most misunderstood and yet thoroughly understood questions of all time. People know why it is enticing yet wonder why they cannot quit. Why is it so alluring? Visual pornography is far more attractive to men than it is for women, but women also struggle with pornography. What is it about pornography that causes us to lose control?

The answer to this is different for men and women. Men become aroused by what they see. God made men this way. It is a normal and healthy aspect of being a male when the object of affection is his wife. Women, on the other hand, desire romance, intimacy, and emotional connection or a relationship. Products are advertised differently to men and women based on what attracts each sex. To get a man's attention, parade before him a woman in a skimpy outfit. To sell to a woman, appeal to her emotions by using puppies, kittens, candlelight tête-à-têtes, or some other mood enticement.

Satan frequently uses visual enticements to tempt us.

Dr. Thomas Politzer wrote, "Research estimates that 80 to 85 percent of our perception, learning, cognition, and activities are mediated through vision."[1] Our eyes are important to us. We use our vision constantly. Obviously, Satan is well aware of this, so he frequently uses visual enticements to tempt us. Solomon wrote, "Thine eyes shall behold strange women, and thine heart shall utter perverse things" (Proverbs 23:33 KJV).

The sex drive was created and placed in humanity by God.

There is absolutely nothing wrong with sex. He told Adam and Eve to be fruitful and multiply—clearly the sex drive was there from the beginning. God created sex to be enjoyed between a man and a woman through marriage. It was never His intent for man or woman to have sex with anyone and everyone, and certainly not the same sex. Therefore, the object of sexual arousal should never be for anyone other than a person's spouse. Dr. Juli Slattery said, "By God's design sex is a powerful force. He created it to be an incredible bonding experience between a husband and wife."[2] Pornography interferes with this bonding.

The word pornography encompasses images and thoughts that both excite and disgust. So why is it so appealing? Porn's intention is to arouse sexual desire. Unlike other vices, pornography plays off of our natural sexual desires and needs. Once again, God placed these natural desires inside of us.

The desire for sex is just as natural as a person's desire for food. However, unlike the need for food, we can survive without sex. We cannot last long without food and water, but we can live our entire lives without sex. That may be extremely challenging, but it is possible.

Society profoundly influences the sex drive—what we see, what we read, where we go, and what we allow into our lives. If we permit improper stimuli, our sex drive will be polluted.

Men struggle with visual, hardcore, sexually explicit pornography. While women can too, they tend to be lured and trapped by romantic and sexually suggestive media. When pornography is consumed, it perverts the natural sex drive into something God did not intend. It feeds the sex drive unnatural and negative images and thoughts. The more porn a person devours, the harder it becomes to break the unhealthy desires. A person rapidly travels a downward spiral.

Pornography and romance novels create the illusion of what a sexual relationship should be. To satisfy that level of desire, one needs more of what created the unhealthy desire in their mind. After a while, the erotica begins to lose its excitement. To regain it, harsher material is needed. For some, they may even act out what they have seen by visiting prostitutes, physically committing adultery, taking advantage of innocent victims, or even committing rape.

More and more women are committing sexual assaults. We used to hear only about men committing them, but there has been a marked increase in female sexual assaults in the last few years. While it is hard to find statistics, female offenders often are not detected or prosecuted.[3] How many female teachers have been arrested for having sexual encounters with underage students in the last several years?

I worked in a large hotel that regularly served as the head-quarters hotel for conventions. One of the hotel restaurants would play a cruel trick to entice guests to eat there. A chef would set up a cooking cart at the entrance of the restaurant and begin roasting garlic and blends of spices. That is all he had to do. He was cooking no actual food. His whole intent was to cause the aroma to waft throughout the hotel. If the guests were not hungry before, just smelling the aroma would cause their mouths to water and their stomachs suddenly let them know how empty they were.

Like the chef roasting the spices, there is no substance to porn. It is an illusion. It titillates the senses but is empty. It cannot satisfy the need for physical connection—only a marital relationship can. Pornography gives the impression that appropriate, godly sex is dull or boring. Pornography is a lie; the truth is porn is bland. It leaves you feeling empty and unsatisfied. It cannot replicate the love shared between marriage partners.

Men, nothing is boring about a healthy sexual relationship with your wife. Women, the same applies to your relationship with your husband. Pornography cannot provide the intimacy that comes from being with a spouse; it cannot offer the personal connection that comes from being vulnerable, close, and familiar. Being in an intimate relationship with our spouse makes us vulnerable, and a trusting, loving, healthy relationship needs that. We are one with our spouse. That connection cannot happen with the performers on a screen or characters in a story. Viewing or reading porn cannot duplicate the love shared between marriage partners.

When my daughter was little, she loved to eat "mean means" (green beans) fed to her from the baby food jar. Have you ever tasted baby food green beans? Don't—unless you like bland, flavorless food. One day my wife cooked fresh green beans for our supper and decided to mash up some to feed to our daughter.

They had bacon, onion, salt, and other seasonings in them. One taste and that was the end of the baby food "mean means." She would never eat the boring green beans again. The real deal was much better than bland, store-bought baby food.

"And the Lord God said, 'It is not good that man should be alone; I will make him a helper comparable to him'" (Genesis 2:18). God knew a hermit-like existence was "not good" for Adam, so He made a companion and helper for him out of his rib. By God's design, Adam and Eve bonded together in a relationship—a lifetime male-and-female relationship as husband and wife.

Pornography can never provide companionship like that. It does not alleviate loneliness; in fact, it compounds it. Stores now sell companion pillows for lonely people. A pillow cannot replace a real person. Porn, like the pillow, is an insufficient substitute for a lifetime partner. It is the porn that is truly bland or boring. Sex was made to be enjoyed by a husband and wife. How can a computer screen compare with that? It cannot. While marriage is not just about a sexual relationship, sex within the confines of marriage can be incredibly satisfying. Part of the equation is learning what each other needs. A man must understand the emotional needs of his wife and connect with her through communication. A man feels connected to his wife through the sexual relationship. Pornography—regardless of the form it takes or the level of intensity—will never replace this.

Porn is not the real world. It is Fantasyland.

Solomon instructs a husband to be satisfied with his wife. "Let her breasts fill you at all times with delight; be intoxicated always in [your wife's] love" (Proverbs 5:19 ESV). Some nameless woman on a page or screen may gratify, delight, and intoxicate a man; however, it is merely an image. A man cannot touch her as he can touch his wife. How can a real woman compete with some woman on a page or a screen who never has bad breath, bed head, bone weariness, or headaches? The reality is we men feel most manly when we are fulfilling the needs of our wife. Porn cannot compare to holding her, feeling the softness of her skin, being her hero, and yes, tolerating each other's bad breath. Porn is not the real world. It is Fantasyland.

Regardless of how much we eat today, our bodies will need food tomorrow. Considering this, some foods are simply unhealthy for us to consume. It would not be wise to eat spoiled meat, rotten eggs, or soured milk. These things can make us physically sick. Porn does the same thing for our sex drive and soul. It is like eating rotten eggs. It does not spice up our sex life; it spoils it.

Porn is like a drug—a quick fix without substance. Dr. Robert Weiss of the Sexual Recovery Institute in Los Angeles stated, "Cyber-sex is the crack cocaine of sexual addiction. It works so quickly and it's so instantly intense."[4] Weiss also said that Internet porn is extremely dangerous because of the "Triple A Engine"—access, affordability, anonymity.[5]

Porn is easily accessible. At one time, a person had to go to the corner gas station, bookstore, or the adult-only section of a video store. They had to leave their home to get a porn fix. Now they can get it anywhere that has an Internet or wireless connection, whether through a computer or a mobile device.

Internet porn is affordable. In fact, it can be found for free. No money has to be spent unless someone wants to spend it. No credit card is needed. You don't have to add your name to a mailing list or search for a store that sells the pornography desired. It is available with the simple click of a mouse.

Porn can be found anonymously. Since they do not have to visit adult bookstores, no one will see them; they can get it without having to show their faces or worrying about someone seeing their car in the parking lot of some sleazy establishment. They do not have to show identification.

Pornography, along with subsequent masturbation and orgasm, causes the body to release powerful chemicals that bring about a euphoric feeling. These chemicals do different things, but they all bring about a very welcome and desired effect.

The chemicals released are epinephrine, dopamine, testosterone, oxytocin, vasopressin, norepinephrine, serotonin, and endogenous opiates, among others. These chemicals are many of the same chemicals found in drugs that addicts use. Opiates and oxytocin are very addictive. Serotonin is the calming chemical; this is why men often feel the need for sleep immediately after sex.[6]

I can still recall the nude image I saw when I was eight.

These sudden surges of hormones and chemicals have a powerful effect on a person. The feeling is intense and very much like a drug high, and the image is burned into the brain. The experience is so intense and exciting that most men can recall the details of their first experience with porn years later. I was eight years old when I saw my first nude image and can still recall where I was and whom I was with. I also remember the first porn video I saw for the same reason.

It has been said that crack cocaine is instantly addictive. Use it once, and a person will crave it forever. Porn is much the same way. Something about it makes it difficult to overcome even when all the dangers are known and understood. Pornography is like crack cocaine. It is not easy to put down once started because of these powerful chemicals, hormones, and the euphoria they cause. Due to the chemical high resulting in an extremely enjoyable experience, most want to repeat the euphoria. This is why so many develop the unhealthy habit of porn usage and masturbation. It is essentially a cheap drug fix.

There is just one problem with this. Just like drugs, the material that produces such an incredible feeling eventually starts to lose its appeal. Harder material is needed to regain that experience. For example, soft porn may work for a while, but eventually the desire for something a bit more explicit takes over. Then a new desire for something even harder is formed. If not stopped, research has shown that many will begin to act out what they have seen, either through an out-of-wedlock affair, visiting a prostitute, or something even worse.[7]

Dr. James Dobson interviewed Ted Bundy the day before he was executed for killing twenty-eight women. Bundy stated, "I've lived in prison for a long time now, and I've met a lot of men who have been motivated to commit violence just like me. And without exception every one of them was deeply involved in pornography, without question, without exception, deeply influenced and consumed by an addiction to pornography."[8]

Once the sex drive is perverted, we have to regain control of it.

The issue with our sex drive is self-control or our lack of it. It takes an extreme amount of discipline to conquer the appetite we have allowed to go unchecked. Once the sex drive is perverted, we have to regain control of it. Our system is used to having this chemical release and yearns for it. It craves the excitement. It wants the surge of adrenaline. It desires the release of sexual tension. It longs for the calming effect. When the sex drive is twisted or perverted, it is quite challenging to overcome these perverse desires.

We will always contend with our sex drive and our fleshly desires. Even though sex is not sinful within a marital relationship, still we must keep it in check. I cannot tell you how many times I begged God to take away my sex drive. I am quite thankful He refrained from answering that request.

More and more women are becoming trapped by the allurement of pornography.

Most of the discussion within this book is directed toward men. However, more and more women are becoming trapped by the allurement of pornography. "By and large, men prefer images and graphic sex sites; women prefer erotic stories and romance sites."[9] Walk into a bookstore and see how many romance novels are displayed.

While studies indicate women can be turned on sexually by sight, they are primarily turned on by touch. Touch can be through physical contact, but more often it is through emotional connection. Many women like to read romance novels because they appeal to their emotions. Harlequin books have been around for years and are written for women. These books are filled with raunchy, uninhibited sexual encounters. Sexy or romantic stories do the same things for women that visual porn does for men. They speak to the emotions of a woman and are intended to entice, excite, arouse, and bring sexual pleasure. The author of *Fifty Shades of Grey* wrote on her website, "Erotic, amusing, and deeply moving, the Fifty Shades Trilogy is a tale that will obsess you, possess you, and stay with you forever."[10]

It is becoming more common to hear of women watching porn. Studies and research are all over the map on this subject. Some say women are viewing it more than ever; others say they are not. Enough studies have been performed to indicate women certainly do view pornography, but the data depend on the findings of various research articles. For example, Top Ten Reviews states 31 percent of women reported using porn. This study surveyed 813 college students ages eighteen to twenty-six, five hundred of them women.[11]

According to Dirty Girls Ministries, 25 percent of Christian women are addicted to pornography.[12] It should be noted the term "Christian" is used in a general sense. Regardless of whether the numbers give an entirely accurate picture, women, including Oneness Apostolic women, have become trapped by pornography, soap operas, love stories, and graphic romance novels and magazines filled with sexual content.

Fantasyland is just as alluring to a woman as it is to a man.

A woman's sex drive is just as important to her as a man's sex drive is to him. God placed that drive within her and gave her a desire to be with a man—her husband. Fantasyland is just as alluring to a woman as it is to a man. Women want to escape from the doldrums and problems of life just as men do, hence the steamy stories.

The principles found in the Word of God are just as useful for overcoming sin in a woman's life as they are in the life of a man. If a woman finds herself trapped by pornography or other erotica, much of the information in this book will apply. Read on! There is hope.

THE LIES OF PORN

The thief does not come except to steal, and to kill, and to destroy. I have come that they may have life, and that they may have it more abundantly (John 10:10).

When [the devil] speaks a lie, he speaks from his own resources, for he is a liar and the father of it (John 8:44).

Satan is a master deceiver. He tempts us with things that are appealing and exciting to our flesh. If we knew the reality of the sin we were being tempted with, would we give in? Temptation will present itself in one of three areas:

For all that is in the world—the lust of the flesh, the lust of the eyes, and the pride of life—is not of the Father but is of the world. And the world is passing away, and the lust of it; but he who does the will of God abides forever (I John 2:16–17).

This world and the lust within will someday pass away. Until then, we need to be on our guard. So where does lust or physical desire come from? What causes it? Simply put, "lust of the flesh" is a sensual, sinful, or evil desire. It is not the same as the desire for sleep when you are tired or for food when you are hungry. One can also have an unhealthy desire to overeat (gluttony) or to be lazy (slothfulness).

If a person's sexual cravings fall outside of biblical boundaries, they are being driven by lustful desires.

Since sex is a natural desire, how can the desire for sex turn from being acceptable into selfish lust? It happens when the desire for sex no longer fits within the parameters of what the Word of God sets as satisfactory. The Word of God specifies a man is to marry one woman. For example, it teaches adultery, fornication, homosexuality, and bestiality are wrong. If a person's sexual cravings fall outside of biblical boundaries, they are being driven by lustful desires.

Thank God, we are not stuck or left alone when we face temptations; we have a way to escape them. Remember temptation is not a sin. It is when the temptation is acted upon improperly, or we give in to it, that sin occurs. When temptations arise, a choice is placed before us.

> But each one is tempted when he is drawn away by his own desires and enticed. Then, when desire has conceived, it gives birth to sin; and sin, when it is full-grown, brings forth death (James 1:14–15).

> No temptation has overtaken you except such as is common to man; but God is faithful, who will not allow you to be tempted beyond what you are able, but with the temptation will also make

the way of escape, that you may be able to bear
it (I Corinthians 10:13).

Let's say you win an all-expense-paid trip to the location of
your choice anywhere in the world. You will ride in a limousine,
be flown on the finest private aircraft, and stay in a five-star hotel. You will receive expensive clothing to wear, have gorgeous
escorts of the opposite sex to accompany you throughout the
trip, and the list goes on.

You decide you want to go to a beautiful tropical island.
When the departure day arrives, someone rings your doorbell
and says, "Are you ready to go?" You answer, "Yes." He hands
you a blindfold and tells you to put it on. You ask why, and
he responds it is part of the deal. You are to wear a blindfold
throughout the entire trip. You raise a fuss, but he shows you the
rules for winning the trip. Sure enough, you must be blindfolded
to participate in the vacation. Somehow you overlooked this rule
when you entered the contest. You reluctantly agree to be blindfolded. He tells you video and photos will be taken so that you
can see everything that happened during the trip.

You take this journey but cannot see anything. Still, you have
an enjoyable time. Everything seems wonderful. The entire trip
is relaxing. The exotic food is delicious. Every need is met and
you can do anything you want without financial worries. Despite
your inability to see, you have an incredible time.

A week after you return home, you receive the video and
pictures. Shockingly, nothing was the way it was supposed to be.
The limo was, in fact, a beat-up taxi. Instead of flying on a private jet, you were flown economy class on a commercial flight.
Instead of the private yacht, you were on an old fishing trawler.
Instead of a five-star hotel, you were in a room that makes Motel
6 look like the Ritz-Carlton. The escorts were anything but gorgeous: the women were old, had greasy hair, and were missing
most of their teeth; the men were slobs wearing stained T-shirts

and looking like they combed their hair with an eggbeater. The sandy beach was filthy and near a nuclear power plant.

The exquisite food promised was dog, opossum, rat, and carp, skillfully seasoned. Your attractive clothes were stained, dirty, and torn. Everything was the exact opposite of what you were told. The entire trip had been a lie! You are upset and frustrated. The thought of what you ate sickens you. You feel cheated, abused, and ashamed. You had planned to show the pictures to your friends, but not now.

A month later, the travel agent calls to tell you that you won another trip. He apologizes for the previous trip and is very sorry about the misunderstanding. He promises the agency will make it up to you; this time everything will be perfect. He is very persuasive. Reluctantly you agree and sign up. Much to your chagrin, the same thing happens.

You fall for the bait-and-switch vacation over and over. Why? You cannot see what is really happening behind the scenes, plus, you are hoping the empty promises will become reality. While your sense of vision is temporarily blinded, your mind plays tricks on you and fills in the mental images, enhancing your perception. You repeat the experience because it was fun; you found temporary enjoyment in the lie.

Sin entices us much the same way. Sin is alluring, but it promises one thing and delivers another. It appears wonderful, but the reality of sin doesn't even come close to our perception of how it will be. We believe feeding lust's desire will satisfy us, but being bound by sin is always far worse than the excitement that temptation offers. Reality never changes. Truth does not vary. What changes is our perception of reality and our under-standing of that bill of goods we've just been sold.

That is what porn does: it sells us a bogus bill of goods—and the reality is far different than what we expect. Satan will ask, "What is your fantasy or desire today? You can have whatever you want." While it appears you get what you want, the reality is far different. Keep reading for the explanation why.

Fantasyland is an imaginary destination you cannot possibly reach.

Fantasyland is our unrealistic expectations and desires. Sometimes we do not like reality so we daydream, wishing for things we cannot have, which makes reality seem much worse than it really is. Fantasyland is an imaginary destination we cannot possibly reach. It is an illusion of our own conjuring fed by the sinful vice in which we choose to partake.

Fantasyland is like a predator that lures its prey. By the time the victim realizes what has happened, it is too late. Similarly, by the time the big bass realizes the bait has a hook in it, it is already snared.

In John 10:10, Jesus warned of "the thief." Question: Who is the thief? Answer: Satan. How can he possibly come in to kill and destroy? First, he does not dress like a thief. He does not act like a thief. His tone is persuasive and sincere. How can a person identify him as a criminal when he looks so great and displays his offer with such enticing word pictures and apparent sincerity? The person eagerly lets him in.

I am reminded of the Sirens in Greek mythology. They appeared as beautiful, naked women who would sing out to sailors passing nearby. But when the sailors would turn toward them, the Sirens were, in fact, sea nymphs who enjoyed killing and destroying the sailors. The sin of pornography desires to devour us. Its Siren song calls out to us.

We think we can get away with playing the game. We "repent" and all is well. We toy with the enemy just as the three little pigs did with the big bad wolf. We sing, "Who's afraid of the big bad wolf?" and believe the little haystack house we built will stop him, but it won't.

The pleasure of sin only temporarily masks the real hunger of the soul.

We also believe that porn won't hurt *this time;* it won't effect us *this time.* We can handle it. However, it leaves us feeling guilty, ashamed, and frustrated with ourselves for giving in—again! The pleasure of sin only temporarily masks the real hunger of the soul. When the excitement is gone, we feel worse than we did before we gave in to our lustful desire.

Pornography lies to us every time we see it or read it. It says sex is acceptable anytime, anywhere, and with anyone we want. It says sex outside of marriage is fine. It tells guys that girls are to look a certain way to be attractive. It says girls will let you do anything you want to them; they are here only to please you sexually. Last, it sells the belief that sex is the ultimate pleasure in life.

Sex in pornography is not based on a genuine relationship. It is acting! The men and women involved are performers. While the sexual act itself is real, most of the time the emotions are faked. They are playing for the camera. The action is not centered on love. It is just about feeling good, and that is debatable. For the actors and actresses, porn is a job. For many of them, sex loses its appeal. Having sex with that many people causes it to become mundane, dangerous, and abusive. The rates of sexually transmitted diseases (STDs) in the porn industry are staggering.

Porn is degrading.

Pornography conveys many lies about women and sex. It is sad that so many believe these lies. Women are referred to as animals, body parts, and playthings. They are objects used for a man's pleasure. Porn is degrading. It is bizarre, kinky, painful, and just plain gross. Women are shown being tortured, humiliated, and completely disrespected.

A typical porn scenario is when she says no she really means yes. Women are shown being raped, fighting and kicking, and then giving in and enjoying it. Porn attempts to make rape sexy and arousing. Women are shown being tied up, beaten, humiliated, yelled at, called horrible names, slapped, and tortured, all with a smile on their faces. Porn teaches that men can hurt and abuse women for entertainment, and the woman will come back for more. Why? She is there solely to submit to a man's every whim.

Porn often suggests that we cannot enjoy sex unless it is weird, illegal, or dangerous. While child porn is illegal, one of the biggest sellers in the porn industry is imitation child porn. Women dress and act like little girls to fulfill a very disturbing fetish. The industry pushes the limits as far as it can.

Porn attempts to make prostitution appear exciting, which is far from reality. How many prostitutes are controlled by others? A pimp dictates their every move. Their dates frequently beat them. Many have been raped and murdered throughout history. Glamorous? I think not.

In pornography sex is nothing more than a game. The woman is meant to be conquered. Sex is often referred to as scoring. Pornography projects the idea that women can be purchased. If you spend money on a woman, she is obligated to have sex with you, much like spending money on a car gives you the right to use it. Many see sex as the end game of every date—it is the ultimate goal. "What do I get in return for my generosity?"

Porn also sells the belief that only women with perfect store-bought curves have value. If a woman is overweight or flawed in any way, she is ridiculed. Porn does not care about a woman's mind, personality, feelings, desires, or education, just her body.

Porn also lies to a woman. It tells her she must look a certain way to be desirable to her husband. The only quality of importance she has is her body. If she does not have an hourglass figure, she will be a turn-off to her husband. Porn will tell her that her husband is comparing her to the porn starlets. It will say men need porn because of a flaw they find in their wives. That may be the case with some men, but the men I have dealt with

never made these comparisons. Men have the ability to com-
partmentalize items inside their brains. The porn goes in one
compartment, and marital sex goes in another.

Porn tells women that men who do not fit a specific profile
are losers. Men must be physically fit to be desirable. They must
be tall, dark, and handsome. They must achieve a certain status
in life to be attractive. Men must be wealthy and hold a position
of power, not to mention being highly educated, and the list goes
on. Ladies who marry successfully must marry a man who fits
this mold . . . lies, lies, lies. Spiritual success is far greater than
any success in this world.

Another fabrication is that pornography is educational. Adam
Glasser, a porn actor and producer, said, "People learn from what
we do. They get educated from what we do. . . . Our movies are
entertainment and education tools. . . . Men have walked up to me
and said, 'I conceived my child to your movies.'"[1]

No one needs porn to explain what to do.

Uh, just one question: how did thousands of years of reproduc-
tion happen without porn? Adam and Eve did not have a sex
manual. God did not give them a copy of *The Joy of Sex* to help
them along. Eve did not need *Cosmopolitan* to list one hundred
sexy moves to please Adam. Sex came naturally to them. No one
needs porn to explain what to do. If you are married, I am quite
confident you figured out what to do on your honeymoon. If you
are not married, when the time comes, you too will figure it out.
It's not complicated.

Worldly values perpetuate many of these lies. The world says
you must dress and act a certain way to be attractive or desired. It is all about appearance and status level. Society does
not consider a person's godliness or spirituality in relation to
their self-worth.

I believe the worst, most dangerous lie, however, is when the porn viewer or reader gets to the point where they rationalize their porn use as being harmless and something they can control. They have arrived at the same place as the alcoholic who believes he or she doesn't have a problem. No amount of intervention or persuasion will convince them. That is when God, and only God, can help—and then, only if He is allowed!

If you are struggling, now is the time to change course. If pornography's chains are binding you, you need help. You need direction. You need God!

If porn is allowed to reign over you, it will distort your view of marriage and sex. It will alter your view of your own self-worth and skew your thoughts toward the opposite sex. Pornography erodes the moral values of those who view it. If a person has a moral standard against alternate lifestyles, homosexual marriage for example, watching porn will undermine their convictions. We have seen a vast increase in homosexuality in our society. Don't think for a minute that pornography hasn't played a huge role in the propagation of this behavior. Author Tyler Kingkade cites a study published in the academic journal *Communication Research*, which "suggests that the more heterosexual men, especially less educated heterosexual men, watch pornography, the more supportive they become of same-sex marriage."[2]

Far too many believe the lies of pornography. Those who believe lies and enjoy evil rather than truth will be damned or condemned to spend eternity in Hell. Be familiar with Satan's evil schemes (II Corinthians 2:11).

Pornography is a lie! We must escape this fantasyland.

> Therefore do not let sin reign in your mortal body,
> that you should obey it in its lusts (Romans 6:12).

We must not allow sin to reign in our bodies. What does the word "reign" mean? It means to *rule over*. We cannot allow sin to rule over us. If sin reigns over us, it will kill and destroy us. Somehow, someway, we must have a transformation of the heart. We must let our minds be renewed (Romans 12:1–2).

8

A LOOK
BEHIND THE SCENES

And this is the condemnation, that the light has come into the world, and men loved darkness rather than light, because their deeds were evil. For everyone practicing evil hates the light and does not come to the light, lest his deeds should be exposed (John 3:19–20).

The thief does not come except to steal, and to kill, and to destroy (John 10:10).

Until now we have discussed porn simply as the portrayal of sexual objects and acts. Let's talk about the industry and expose it, for lack of a better term. I must warn you that to do so I will be sharing some very disturbing realities. I do not do this for shock value but to uncover the truth that much of what the porn industry portrays is phony and fake. There is very little that is real about it. In fact, the industry tries extremely hard to hide the painful truth of their debauched, sordid world. Sin is always sold in a beautifully decorated package that is very tempting, but the bait Satan uses is lies and deception. The porn industry is no exception; it has a horrific side.

What an exciting job it would be to be in that industry. Those guys are so lucky. This thought went through my mind many times while I was viewing porn. Porn actors get to have sex with gorgeous babes and get paid for it! Furthermore, the supply of new girls who practically throw themselves at you is never-ending. What red-blooded male would not want that job?

The glitz and glamor of pornography is a shameless façade. It is like a billboard splashed with glossy pictures and tantalizing messages. But what you see is not what you get. This industry has a disgustingly sick and twisted dark side lurking in the shadows.

The industry despises the actual word "pornography" due to the negative connotations. For instance, in the *Los Angeles Times*, Ralph Frammolino and P. J. Huffstutter cited Steven Hirsch, founder and co-chairman of Vivid Entertainment, who said, "Pornography has always been a bad word, and we're not about bad words. We're about making money."[1]

Reality tells an entirely different story.

The industry prefers the term "Adult Entertainment." It has a much cleaner sound. The whole industry likes to portray itself with a sanitized view, kind of like a hospital. An average person rarely sees the ugly side of a hospital with the blood and guts. We see clean floors and spotless linens and smell antiseptic and flowers. Which term sounds more appealing to you, "pornography" or "adult entertainment"? It is just part of the facade. They want you to believe it is clean and safe, a healthy environment full of happy people—a delightful industry whose whole purpose is to entertain adults. Sounds harmless, right? Reality tells an entirely different story.

I want to show you what happens behind the camera. No, it is not just costume changes and a big party. I hope this information changes your view of this industry. This information comes from research, testimonies of former insiders, and news stories that have trickled out.

Have you ever had the experience of pushy salespeople trying to sell you an item you do not want? They circle like vultures. With slick tactics and smooth talk, they attempt to sell you something you "cannot live without." If you show a smidgeon of interest, they drool and try to upsell. They will do whatever they must do to get your money. They may tell you a sob story about their sick child at home who is starving. They may say they are just one or two sales away from winning a vacation. (Why doesn't the buyer ever get the trip?) They often use high-pressure tactics: "This deal is only good today. It will not last until tomorrow. If you want this, you have to buy right now. Why wait?"

The producers of pornography are much like the salespeople. Their objective is to get the newest hottie to do all sorts of sexual acts by the quickest means possible. The more perverted, the better. Her well-being does not matter. She has body parts to exploit through DVDs, magazines, and website memberships. Bob Guccione, founder and former publisher of *Penthouse* magazine, stated, "Unlike most guys, when I see a pretty girl the thing that I immediately think of is not how she looks to me, but how she would look to my readership. In other words, what is her centerfold potential?[2]

Pornographers prey on unsuspecting females. They entice them with flattery. Shelley Lubben, a former porn actress wrote, "A few compliments later and a nice-sized financial offer, we find ourselves standing in the middle of a porn agent's office being talked out of 'nude modeling' and into anal sex."[3]

Coercion tactics are common practice in the industry.

Imagine getting a job and being told you had to do only one thing—take off your clothing. Then when you do, demands are made to force you into doing something you never wanted to do. Instead of just taking photos, they want to shoot a video.

"Have sex with this person and we'll video it. Hey, you want to make real money? Why don't you do this sex act? If you don't, you won't get paid." Coercion tactics are common practice in the industry.

The horror stories should get our attention. First, STDs run rampant in the industry, although they try very hard to hide this fact. According to Dr. Sharon Mitchell, 66 percent of porn performers have Herpes, 12–28 percent have STDs, and 7 percent have HIV. Chlamydia and gonorrhea, "along with hepatitis, seem to stick to everything."[4] Chloe, a porn actress, stated, "After you've been in this business for a while, you have herpes. Everyone has herpes."[5]

A September 2009 report by the Los Angeles Department of Public Health cited 2,396 cases of Chlamydia, 1,389 cases of gonorrhea, and five syphilis cases among porn performers. The study indicated that industry performers had a 20 percent higher infection rate than the general public.[6] One report stated, "LA porn stars have significantly higher rates of sexually transmitted diseases (STDs) than legal prostitutes in Nevada."[7]

"The director didn't really care how I felt; he only wanted to finish the video."

The industry is abusive and humiliating. It runs the gamut of *vanilla* sex to physical cruelty. Harsher sex scenes are becoming more of the norm in the business. Regan Starr described an abusive scene in which she participated: "I was told before the video—and they said this very proudly, mind you—that in this line most of the girls start crying because they're hurting so bad. . . . I couldn't breathe. I was being hit and choked."[8] In another interview about the same scene, she added, "So what they did was leave the crying and the kicking and the screaming in when I was saying, 'Stop the cameras' because this man was hurting me. He tossed me over his shoulder and was using hard fists and slapped me. . . . Grabbed me by the throat and grabbed me by the neck and I was choking."[9]

Another actress, Genevieve, described an experience she had during a shoot. "The abuse and degradation was rough. I sweated and was in deep pain. On top of the horrifying experience, my whole body ached, and I was irritable the whole day. The director didn't really care how I felt; he only wanted to finish the video."[10]

Michelle, a twenty-year-old actress, said her male partner got rough with her while filming a scene. He slapped her face violently and choked her. Afterward, she looked shaken; her face was red and her eyes were watery. She said, "I look torn up—can you tell? I took a beating today, and it was great."

On one video shoot, Michelle's director convinced her to have sex with twelve male actors in prison outfits. She attempted to back out to no avail. She stated, "It was really hard because I really felt like a piece of meat . . . in a lion's cage, twelve lions. . . . I had to do a lot of things I can't imagine anyone wanting to do." She said afterward she couldn't stop crying. She packed her bags and moved back home to Utah. Unfortunately, she later returned to the industry.[11]

Elizabeth did a scene with twenty-five male actors. She felt pressured by porn producers to film this scene. She stated, "I never thought I would have done something like that. I felt disgusted and violated, but what was I going to do? I had three children, and I desperately needed the money." She fasted for two days and drank heavily the day before filming. She stated, "I kept saying to myself, 'This is going to be over in an hour.' I wanted to break down and cry, but I hid behind my fake smile. During the movie, I mentally and emotionally checked out and felt like I died." Elizabeth went on to say, "My body was sore the next couple days, and I wasn't right mentally for two weeks after that. I wasn't able to use the bathroom right either. My internal system was totally messed up."[12]

During an interview, Kami Andrews said she liked the attention but did not like having abnormal bowel movements. "You are constantly doing enemas, and you're fasting, and you're taking all these different pills, [Ex-Lax], and it [messes] up your internal system."[13] When asked about the prevalence of abortions in the industry, she stated, "I had one."[14]

In an interview with the *Christian Post*, Shelley Lubben, a former actress, said, "It's common for porn stars to get abortions; it's very common for them to have stress disorder."[15]

Girls are merely used as sex objects. Their bodies serve one purpose: sexual pleasure for the consumer. That is it. They have no real value outside of the sexual pleasure they can bring to a man. Their feelings, desires, wants, and needs are not considered.

This is just what the industry wants, however. They want some unsuspecting, young female to come along and then devour them like a lion preying on a defenseless animal. "Amateurs come across better on screen. Our customers feel that. Especially by women you can see it. They still feel strong pain," said Carlo Scalisi, owner of 21 Sexury Video.[16]

John Stagliano, a porn actor and producer, stated of filming another male performer, "Together we evolved toward rougher stuff. He started to spit on girls. A strong male-dominant thing, with women being pushed to their limit. It looks like violence, but it's not. I mean, pleasure and pain are the same thing, right?"[17]

Claire, a twenty-year-old performer, had been in the industry for three months. During one scene, two men were using her in horrible ways, causing her pain. This led to the following exchange:

Man: "Are you crying?"

Claire: "No, I'm enjoying it."

Man: "[Expletive deleted], I thought you were crying. It was turning me on when I thought you were crying."

Claire: "Would you like me to?"

Man: "Yea, give me a [expletive deleted] tear. Oh, there's a [expletive deleted] tear."[18]

I recall seeing a disgusting scene in which a young woman was crying from pain. Did the man stop? Did he ask if she was okay? Was he concerned about her comfort or feelings? Nope! He laughed at her repeatedly while continuing the degrading acts.

"It's not good for a girl to stick around that long anyhow. It's not good for her mental health."

Chester Anuszak, an actor, said a woman's turnaround time in porn is much faster than a man's. Women are phased out much quicker because viewers want to see a constant stream of new female faces. He said, "It's not good for a girl to stick around that long anyhow. It's not good for her mental health." He said of being filmed having sex, "It's still awkward. It always is. It's not meant to be that way, you know. So it is awkward."[19]

Luke Ford, an Internet gossip columnist on the adult entertainment industry, declared, "Most girls who enter this industry do one video and quit. The experience is so painful, horrifying, embarrassing, humiliating for them that they never do it again."[20] On average, an actress in adult films has a career length of roughly one year.[21]

Drug and alcohol abuse is common with the performers. They use these substances to cope with the abuse, degradation, and shame. One actress noted, "Everybody is on drugs. It's an empty lifestyle trying to fill up a void."[22] Porn star Jenna Presley said she thinks 90 percent of people in the business take drugs or alcohol, but maybe 70 percent have a problem.[23] It is also common for someone to offer alcohol and painkillers to porn actresses to numb and prepare them for agonizing and degrading sex acts. They are sent to industry doctors for anti-anxiety drugs to help them cope with what they face. They are prescribed Vicodin, Xanax, and Valium among other drugs.[24]

"You're viewed as an object—not as a human with a spirit."

Tanya Burleson, a performer, said, "Guys are punching you in the face. You get ripped. Your insides can come out of you. It's never ending. You're viewed as an object—not as a human with a spirit. People do drugs because they can't deal with the way they're being treated."[25]

The word *demoralizing* is insufficient to describe the sheer emotional and psychological trauma that many of these girls go through. Then consider the physical abuse and suffering. Some of them suffer terror and very violent acts. If someone committed these acts outside of this legal industry, they would be arrested for assault. Do you think their agents are there to protect them? Think again. The agents do not care about the girls. Agents are part of the industry that consumes them. The girls are left to fend for themselves. Imagine a cat in a room full of vicious dogs. In essence, that frequently happens on porn shoots.

What about the money? Do the performers rake in the cash? No, not unless they are willing to take significant risks and allow themselves to be used in disgraceful and tragic ways. Even then, they receive little. The pay for an in-demand actress ranges from $800 to $4,000 depending on the scene and what sexual activities occur.[26] These actresses usually have contracts spelling out what their pay will be and in which activities they will and will not participate. The average newbie will make $250 to $1,250 per scene, depending on what acts she performs.[27]

Who rakes in the cash? The pornography companies, by the billions. In 2007, global porn revenues were estimated at $20 billion, with $10 billion in the United States. The Free Speech Coalition estimated both global and US porn revenues have been reduced by 50 percent between 2007 and 2011, due to the amount of free pornography available online.[28]

Do you still think it is a harmless industry? Do you still think pornography is romantic, loving, exotic, incredibly exciting, or even educational? What exactly does it teach? Does it teach men to treat women properly? Do you still think they care about their performers? Let's talk about the suicides and untimely deaths.

I remember envying Chester Anuszak. He got to have sex with so many beautiful women, and he was paid to do so. What a life! He was living my fantasy. How lucky could a guy be? His life must not have been what I thought it was. He hanged himself at the age of forty-three. His porn actress wife discovered his body in a closet in his home.[29] So much for my porn hero. Turns out being a porn star was not all that fulfilling in the long run.

What about Shannon Michelle Wilsey? She shot herself at the age of twenty-three. Adult Video News has her ranked at number nineteen of the top fifty porn stars of all time.[30]

At the age of twenty-six, Michelle Schei died of a self-inflicted gunshot wound to the head. She left behind a note giving the impression she could no longer cope with personal problems.[31]

Nineteen-year-old Alyssa Funke shot herself with a shotgun after making her first porn video. She was a straight-A student at the University of Wisconsin at River Falls. She had everything going for her and had a great future. The belief is she killed herself after former high school classmates taunted her because of the porn video.[32]

What would a dead porn star say if they could come back for five minutes?

A number of porn stars have died from AIDS, drug overdoses, or alcohol poisoning. Out of about two thousand performers in the industry in California, 207 have died from AIDS, suicide, homicide, drugs, or premature deaths between 2003 and 2014. That is a very high percentage rate. The average life expectancy of a performer is only 37.43 years compared to the average life expectancy of Americans at 78.1 years.[33] What stable-minded human would want to support an industry that cut people's lives in half? What would a dead porn star say if he or she could come back for five minutes?

Obviously, this is just a small sample of instances, but there are numerous tragic testimonies associated with this "elite" industry. Time and space do not permit the telling of each sordid tale. Satan desires to destroy lives. He will take everything a person has and more. Porn is not a harmless, victimless industry.

What about the male actors? They have a constant parade of fresh young "babes," which should get the guys aroused and ready to go, but the frequency of sexual performances interrupts and interferes with their systems too. The men often have to use enhancement drugs, such as Viagra, to help them "perform." Industry insiders say nearly 90 percent of new actors use drugs.[34] In extreme cases, drugs are administered by injection into the base of the male organ. The injection sites do not always have time to stop bleeding before filming commences, which creates a biohazard concern. However, it is often overlooked.

The cliché "It's all fun and games until someone gets hurt" applies here perfectly. It appears to be fun, exciting, enjoyable, and even desirable. Everyone seems to love working in this industry; however, the opposite is true. It is perverted, offensive, abusive, harmful, and shameful. While the sexual acts are real, everything else is phony. It is called acting for a reason.

Who has all the fun? My guess is the producers who rake in the money. Who gets the most enjoyment? It is enjoyable to those who like to abuse *willing* girls, although some derive pleasure if they are *unwilling*. Last of all, it is enjoyable to the consumers who perpetuate the need for the industry.

They are pressured into vile and extreme acts because, sadly, that's what sells.

The truth is the industry uses women for the voyeuristic desires and pleasures of the audience and the physical desires of abusive producers. As long as the female initially consents, of course, but they are regularly coerced into deeds far beyond what they consented to do. They are pressured into vile and extreme acts because, sadly, that's what sells.

The moment they become legal, the industry tries to lure girls into the debauchery of sin-sick, twisted acts. These girls think, "I like sex and can make a quick buck. I'll be famous. I'll be desired by many." What they do not realize is the industry preys on their naivety and then consumes them as a predator does its victim. Satan, like a roaring lion, devours them.

The depths of despair these girls find themselves in is like peering through the gates of Hell. They suffer psychological abuse in addition to physical violence. When did cruelty and violence become sexy and erotic?

If you are reading this book and are involved in this industry, I want you to know there is hope for you. Jesus Christ loves you and died on the cross for you. He is a place of safety and refuge for all. Jesus conquered death and Hell for lost humanity. That includes you. Your life is valuable. It has worth. Jesus desires to heal your broken heart, and restore to you what Satan has stolen and destroyed.

Cigarette ads do not mention lung cancer. Beer ads do not show broken homes and liver disease. Casino ads fail to tell of those who have gone bankrupt, losing everything they have. Likewise, the porn industry does not like its dirty laundry aired. It keeps its backstory hidden.

Reality does not compare to the fantasyland portrayed.

All of the above proves my point: the reality of porn is in stark contrast to the industry's persona. So much for it being a loving act performed in a pleasant, clean, healthy, romantic environment. And this information has just scratched the surface. Much more sleaze and repulsiveness could be shared, as in twisted, degrading, filthy, disgusting, and perverted. The truth is reality does not compare to the fantasyland portrayed. That broken, wounded girl is someone's daughter and maybe a sister. Some of these women are mothers. Consider the damage caused the next time you are tempted to view porn. Why would anyone choose pain and suffering? It is because temptation is subtle and deceptive. Make the better choice. Decide not to become a victim of their exploitation. Refuse to be a porn user.

CHOOSE THIS DAY

There is no fear in love; but perfect love casts out fear, because fear involves torment. But he who fears has not been made perfect in love (I John 4:18).

No temptation has overtaken you except such as is common to man; but God is faithful, who will not allow you to be tempted beyond what you are able, but with the temptation will also make the way of escape, that you may be able to bear it (I Corinthians 10:13).

In Joshua's final address to the children of Israel at Shechem, he implored them to make the choice to live for God. He said, "And if it seems evil to you to serve the Lord, choose for yourselves this day whom you will serve, whether the gods which your fathers served that were on the other side of the River, or the gods of the Amorites, in whose land you dwell. But as for me and my house, we will serve the Lord" (Joshua 24:15).

His declaration demands a response from us today. It is time to make a decision. Will you continue to serve your flesh or will you reject porn and turn to God? Making up your mind to do right is the biggest part of the battle.

The principles needed to gain freedom from pornography are the same principles needed to break the chains of any sin.

Paul mentioned a way to escape temptation in I Corinthians 10:13. I often prayed to the Lord, "How do I get free from this?" I desperately wanted to discover the way to escape. The exit was there; I just needed to find it, and eventually I did. The principles needed to gain freedom from pornography are the same principles needed to break the chains of any sin or vice known to man. Although this book deals specifically with porn, you can apply these principles of spiritual warfare to any temptation with which you're struggling. Unfortunately, during my fight I wasn't applying the principles correctly.

Here are a couple of analogies to help clarify this. You are out hunting deer, and you have your favorite rifle at your side. A ten-point buck walks into your area and is within range. You pick up the gun, aim, and pull the trigger, but nothing happens. Why? Did you load it? Did you use the proper ammunition? Is the safety on? When you are ready to fire, you must have the correct ammunition, the rifle must be loaded, and the safety must be turned off.

Think of your house. It is wired for electricity. All that power is useless if you fail to flip on the light switch or plug in the refrigerator. The power is available and usable. We need to take advantage of it for it to fulfill its intended purpose. We have to plug in to activate the power.

God has given us all the tools necessary to defeat the enemy.

The Holy Ghost will guide us into all truth (John 16:13), but His power is worthless if we do not correctly put it to use. How can we defeat the enemy if we do not have the Word of God in our heart? God has given us all the tools necessary to defeat the enemy. It is our job to use them.

> His divine power has given us everything we need for life and godliness through our knowledge of him who called us by his own glory and goodness. Through these he has given us his very great and precious promises, so that through them you may participate in the divine nature and escape the corruption in the world caused by evil desires (II Peter 1:3–4 NIV).

Several factors must be examined. First, we must regain control of our sex drive. How do we do that? One of the biggest problems with most porn viewers and readers is they have a hard time admitting they have a problem with it. The primary reason for this is because of the tremendous fear one faces— fear of rejection by their spouse, peers, family, and church. They just know that if they admit to having a problem with porn, they will lose absolutely everything. They must come to the realization that they have a problem and need help. They must admit that problem!

Another factor is society's influence that constantly tells us sex outside of marriage is the norm. Pornography is okay. Whatever your sexual fantasy is, go for it. Yet what society says is in direct contrast to what the Word of God says.

If you cannot talk about it, you will not overcome it!

I am certainly not saying people do not face fear when opening up about other sins, but porn habits are hard for Christians to admit. It is a difficult subject for Christians because many view it as taboo. I know from experience that if you cannot talk about it, you will not overcome it!

While the subject of perverted sex strikes fear in most Christians, I find it remarkable that Paul was not afraid to deal with the issue. He named some gross sins in his letters to the churches. Furthermore, the letters were to be read openly to the congregations. Paul was not scared or intimidated. He did not deem the discussion of sexual sins to be off limits; in fact, he often listed sexual sins first when recording unrighteous behaviors. Understandably, we do not want to be graphic or vulgar, but we cannot push these issues aside. (See I Corinthians 6:9–11; II Corinthians 12:21; Galatians 5:19–21.)

I felt as if I were living in a cave all by myself. Surely I was the only man in the church who was hooked on porn. I was smart enough to know others had looked at porn, but I sincerely believed I was the only one bound by it. No one knew my secret struggle. No one could be where I was. I was alone in my misery. I felt isolated, which is exactly what sin does to a person. It isolates us, places tremendous fear in us, and makes us feel rejected. Since it was rarely mentioned while growing up, the lack of teaching on the subject just pushed me further into my little world.

We have to learn how to put our sex drive under proper control and how to rid ourselves of the perversion.

When the sex drive is perverted, it is extremely difficult to overcome the perversion. The Holy Ghost will not erase the images of porn or past experiences from our memory. The Holy Ghost does not control our sexual appetite. We must learn how to put our sex drive under proper control and how to rid ourselves of the perversion. The Holy Ghost will help us, but we will fight this one on our own. It takes a concerted effort on our part to win this war. We must use self-discipline!

"To sin or not to sin? That is the question."

Sin is a choice. When we face temptation, we face a choice. So often, we just give in without putting up any resistance. The reality is we choose to give in. It is a choice whether we are addicted or bound. We are to be stewards over everything God gave us, including our sex drive. This means He also gave us the responsibility of keeping it under control. Either we control it, or it controls us. We have no other option.

No one accidentally sins. Temptation may pop up out of no-where, but we make the choice to give in or resist. To repurpose a line from Shakespeare, "To sin or not to sin? That is the question."

We often overuse and even misuse the word *addiction*. For this reason, I prefer using words like *craving* or *habit*. A person has a porn habit. A *habit* is defined as "1. A usual way of behaving; something that a person does often in a regular and repeated way. 2. a strong need to use a drug, to smoke ciga-rettes, etc."[1]

The word *addiction* is commonly used as an excuse to continue to sin. We use it to imply that we commit sin without choice and that we are not responsible for our actions. This first occurred in the Garden of Eden when God asked Adam if he had sinned. He pointed at Eve, and Eve pointed at the serpent. They passed the blame instead of taking responsibility for their own actions. The word *habit* implies personal responsibility.

Many do the same thing today. "It is not my fault I can't let go of pornography. I am addicted. I cannot be held responsible for what I do." I've heard this same excuse with other vices.

"Alcoholism is a disease."

"I go to casinos because they took my money and I have to win it back."

"I am a serial killer because my mother spanked me with a switch when I was little."

"I am a bank robber because my dad ran off before I was born."

These things are sins. We cannot excuse personal, sinful behavior because some psychologist deems the person's behavior is the normal result of circumstances and/or people who mistreated or neglected the person early in life. The patient is a victim, so the responsibility for his or her behavior lies elsewhere. It is much easier on the psyche for a person to point fingers and pass the blame to something or someone else for his or her own wrongdoing.

Sin is sin regardless of what alternate label is used for it—addiction, craving, habit, compulsion, obsession. Sin is a choice we make. We choose to drink alcohol. Our body may crave it, but we decide to take every sip. We want to light up that cigarette. Our body may scream for the nicotine, but we make that choice to smoke. Pornography is the same. Our body says it needs a sexual fix. We are tense and need to relax. All we have to do is get online and take a quick peek. What is wrong with giving in to the craving? What is wrong with desiring to have a sexual high? This is how our body is made, right? We tell ourselves we can blame it on God for giving us the craving. We can blame it on being addicted. We have to have porn. We can't help it.

> But each one is tempted when he is drawn away
> by his own desires and enticed. Then, when desire
> has conceived, it gives birth to sin; and sin, when it
> is full-grown, brings forth death (James 1:14–15).

We face the moment of decision every single time we face temptation.

In between the temptation and conception is that tiny little point of decision. Temptation is not a sin. It is the point when

options present themselves to us. Every time we face temptation, the decision we make will determine if we will give in or
stand our ground—whether we surrender to sin or whether we
win the battle over temptation. Every man is tempted. We all
face temptations. Even Jesus was tempted.

I was at that point when I drove around to buy condoms
before my date with the cute girl in high school for my JROTC
Military Ball. I was facing extreme temptation. What to do? Give
in or resist? I bravely withstood the temptation, and I am so
thankful I did.

Human nature automatically follows the point of least resistance, which is why it is so easy to choose to sin. Often, a
man will face the temptation to look at porn and doesn't even
consider saying no to his flesh. He bypasses self-discipline. He
certainly doesn't allow the Holy Ghost to lead him. Then he gets
to the point where he blames God for his lack of deliverance.

I find Adam's response somewhat interesting when God
asked him if he had eaten of the tree: "The woman whom *You*
gave to be with me, she gave me of the tree, and I ate" (Genesis
3:12). Did you notice that Adam was not only pointing his finger
at Eve, but he also was placing the ultimate blame on God. "The
woman You gave me offered me the forbidden fruit and I ate it."

> Let no one say when he is tempted, 'I am tempt-
> ed by God'; for God cannot be tempted by evil,
> nor does He Himself tempt anyone (James 1:13).

We must take responsibility for our own actions.

It is not God's fault we find ourselves in a sinful condition. Nor
is it anyone else's fault. We are the one who committed the sin.
It is our fault. No more blaming it on being addicted. No more
blaming it on the kid that first showed us porn. No more blaming

it on anyone other than ourselves. We must take responsibility for our own actions! We will never gain the victory if we do not.

Most temptation comes from the enemy, but what we do with it is our responsibility. If we choose to give in, sin becomes our fault. If we choose to resist, we will be blessed with victory. And it will be easier to overcome the next time we face it!

From experience I can say the worst danger is when a person gets to the point they rationalize porn as being harmless and something they can control. It is the same rationale behind an alcoholic's claim that he or she does not have a problem. No amount of persuasion or intervention will convince that kind of person that they need help. Only God can break the chains of these misguided thoughts. Sadly, some will tune God out and decide they'd rather stay bound in chains. Sin cannot be controlled; it must be fought and conquered with God's help!

Sin binds us and sells us into slavery. Paul wrote, "Do you not know that if you present yourselves as obedient slaves, you are slaves of the one you obey, either of sin resulting in death, or obedience resulting in righteousness?" (Romans 6:16 NET).

It is time to repent, to turn away from sin. The prerequisite for repentance is recognizing one's condition as a sinner. Second, repentance is not just asking God to forgive sin; it is making a conscious decision to leave sin behind and do what is right. This is the point where we decide we want to be free from the bondage of sin. Third, we must realize our role in overcoming sin. This is not entirely up to God. He will do His part, but we must do our part. Do we want to be a slave to sin or be obedient to God and live in righteousness? God *will not* do for us what we *must* do for ourselves!

After we admit our problem and repent, we need an accountability partner. We need someone to fight with us, someone to whom we answer. Not only is the very thought of checking in with some a great deterrent to giving in to temptation, the understanding and strength received from that partner helps alleviate the fear and isolation.

Fear does not come from God. Fear is the padlock that keeps people bound by pornography or any other addiction. Pornography is the chain of sin, but fear prevents the chain from being broken. Speaking to a trusted friend dispels that fear and opens the lock so the chains of pornography can be removed.

The most effective way to keep from falling into sin is to get the Word of God in our heart. The psalmist said, "Your word have I hidden in my heart, that I might not sin against You" (Psalm 119:11).

Memorize scriptural passages that deal specifically with sexual sins. When faced with temptation, quote them. God's Word is powerful! Like a two-edged sword, it cuts to the root of the problem; it discerns the thoughts and intents of the heart. It is the only thing that can defeat the lies of sin and temptation. Understand the weapons of God, and use them correctly.

> But put on the Lord Jesus Christ, and make no provision for the flesh, to fulfill its lusts (Romans 13:14).

Do not make provisions for the flesh. The New Living Translation renders this verse, "Don't let yourself think about ways to indulge your evil desires." In other words, don't be foolish enough to put yourself in a position where you know you'll give in to sin. To make provision for the flesh is to purposefully allow or even invite temptation to arise. Provision says, "I'm doing this just in case." For instance, if I had purchased the condoms, I most likely would have used one. I would have made a provision, just in case.

Pornography will always defeat us if we play the game.

Speaking of pornography, how do we make provisions for our flesh? We flirt with the idea of viewing it. We visit borderline websites. We stay up late to "work" while the rest of the family goes to bed. We sneak around to find opportunities to see it. We go to friends' houses where we know we will see it. Any of these tactics is a sure way to mess up. Thus "making provision for the flesh" is the same as giving yourself a sure way to sin. We plan to sin by making the provision. It's like gambling in a casino; the house always wins. Pornography will always defeat us if we play the game.

> I will set nothing wicked before my eyes; I hate
> the work of those who fall away (Psalm 101:3).

We have to keep ourselves in check. We do this by putting on the Lord Jesus Christ. We cannot flirt with porn or give in to its allurement. Pornography is captivating; once a person has seen it, the desire to see it again will haunt them. Protect yourself against it. Don't set any wicked, vile, or vulgar thing before your eyes. That means magazines, books, movies, graphic or violent video games, or anything that causes the imagination to run unrestricted. The word *wicked* refers to anything that is unholy. Don't allow unholy things into your life.

Jesus wants us to be free from all sin, not just the sins we don't like.

I learned a valuable lesson in my fight for freedom. God wants us to have complete freedom. He is not interested in us having limited or partial freedom. What good would it do to be free in one area but bound in another? Remember Jesus wants us to be free from all sin, not just the sins we don't like. Temptation can be avoided by removing anything ungodly from your home.

The Internet is a valuable tool and is almost necessary in to-day's society. But if you're struggling with temptation, you may have to give up access to the Internet. Jesus spoke of this princi-ple in Matthew 18:8: "If your hand or foot causes you to sin, cut it off and cast it from you. It is better for you to enter into life lame or maimed, rather than having two hands or two feet, to be cast into the everlasting fire."

You can survive without the Internet. People have lived for centuries without it. Will it be easy? No, but look at the alterna-tive. If you absolutely must have Internet access, use a filter and let your spouse or accountability partner set the password.

However, please do not rely solely on a filter to protect you. Although filters are beneficial and will keep you from viewing inappropriate material, they are not foolproof. Some filters do a better job than others. One of the best options is a filter that automatically sends an email to your accountability partner. The safest thing to do is combine a filter with other tools. Some fil-ters have apps that allow you to filter content on mobile devices, smartphones, or tablets. That is also an excellent idea. Whatever you can do to assist in overcoming is beneficial.

As with any tool, a filter will not work if your intent is to see porn. If you want it, you will find it regardless of what tools are available. The tools are simply extras that help stop you from head-ing down the wrong path. It is your choice; what will you decide?

You may not be victorious every time you face temptation. You may fall, but do not stay down! Get back up and fight again. With God's help and strength and by using the tools available, you will make progress.

If you fall, examine the reason. Retrace your steps to de-termine what you did or did not do that led to the mishap. Do not beat yourself up for falling! If you do sin, that failure is not final. Every failure should give you more resolve to fight harder and prepare for victory the next time. The failure can become a success if you learn from it. Celebrate victories! Do not wallow in defeats.

Fight one battle at a time, one day at a time. You cannot have victory today if you are focused on tomorrow before it gets here. In the Lord's Prayer, Jesus instructed us to ask for our daily bread (Matthew 6:11). We need the Word of God every day! Our spiritual life depends on it. Jesus also stated, "If anyone desires to come after Me, let him deny himself, and take up his cross daily, and follow Me" (Luke 9:23). This is a daily walk. We must focus on today, not tomorrow.

As for any battle, you must prepare ahead of time. Armed US fighter jets are on constant alert status at strategic points around the country. They are ready to take to the skies to defend the nation at a moment's notice. We need to prepare ourselves the same way.

> Be self-controlled and alert. Your enemy the devil prowls around like a roaring lion looking for someone to devour. Resist him, standing firm in the faith, because you know that your brothers throughout the world are undergoing the same kind of sufferings (I Peter 5:8–9, NIV).

The King James Version says, "Be sober, be vigilant." You must be on constant guard because the enemy of your soul is out to destroy you. Never let your guard down! It is imperative to have a consistent prayer life and use the tools you have at your disposal.

Unmarried men and women, you can be victorious over pornography and sexual sins.

Single people often have free time. You need to use that time to focus your attention on the things of God. Now is the time to learn to pray and study your Bible. Develop a relationship with Jesus Christ. Instead of filling your time with video games, social media, and other forms of entertainment, spend it learning the

Word of God. Paul told young Timothy, "Be diligent to present yourself approved to God, a worker who does not need to be ashamed, rightly dividing the word of truth" (II Timothy 2:15). The King James Version uses the word *study*. It means to set your heart upon—be diligent, hurry, rush, and seek the approval of God. If you develop healthy habits now, you will learn to conquer your sinful appetites. Unmarried men and women, you can be victorious over pornography and sexual sins. It is no more challenging for you than anyone else.

This battle is worth fighting, and you will overcome if you keep fighting! Keep your focus. If you are battling this, I want you to know you are not alone. You are not a loser, a failure, or a reject. Victory is yours if you want it. If Jesus can save a wretch like me, He can save you too.

Be encouraged and filled with hope. You can gain victory over sin and temptation. Jesus loves you unconditionally. His death on Calvary was for your salvation. Stand up and keep fighting.

THE ACCOUNTABILITY PARTNER

> *Brethren, if a man is overtaken in any trespass, you who are spiritual restore such a one in a spirit of gentleness, considering yourself lest you also be tempted. Bear one another's burdens, and so fulfill the law of Christ* (Galatians 6:1–2).
>
> *A gossip betrays a confidence, but a trustworthy man keeps a secret* (Proverbs 11:13, NIV).

If you have done your homework, you have already confessed to God and repented. Now you need to find someone to whom you can be accountable. Weight-watchers trying to lose weight, for example, step on the scale once a week. Knowing that reckoning day is coming will keep them faithful to their goal. The same principle applies to an accountability partner. The inidividual will be a valuable tool if utilized properly.

First, let's talk about what it means to be accountable. Accountability is defined as "the quality or state of being accountable;

especially: an obligation or willingness to accept responsibility or to account for one's actions."[1]

Second, to be accountable to someone means you give an account of your actions to another person. You need to be honest, accept responsibility, and be willing to admit when you are wrong. This is vital because it forces you to be open with what you do.

Third, I want to define what accountability partners are and how they will help you. These are people to whom you voluntarily confide, and who will assist you in this fight. They will have permission to ask personal questions and invade your comfort zone. They will uphold you in prayer, talk to you about your struggles, point out pitfalls, and help you overcome. It is important to live as an open book before them since they provide an extra set of hands, eyes, and protection in your struggle.

Your accountability partner should be someone trustworthy. Although it can be a peer, I recommend a person whom God has placed in a position of authority in your life such as a pastor, youth pastor, parent, or another ministerial leader. If you are a pastor, choose a man outside of your church, possibly a former pastor or even a Christian counselor.

> Confidence in an unfaithful man in time of trouble is like a broken tooth, and a foot out of joint (Proverbs 25:19).

> A gossip betrays a confidence, but a trustworthy man keeps a secret (Proverbs 11:13, NIV).

Choose someone who understands what confidentiality and discretion mean!

No one likes a toothache. The discomfort and pain can be excruciating. Likewise, placing trust or confidence in a person who is untrustworthy or unfaithful to you can be an equally painful experience. Your accountability partner must be willing to keep your spiritual battle in confidence. I cannot stress this enough—choose someone who understands what confidentiality and discretion mean! We do not want to reveal the most intimate secret within our heart to a gossip.

Verify that they have the time and are willing to hold you accountable. If they cannot, find someone else! Do not use this as an excuse not to be accountable.

Ladies, your accountability partner should meet the same qualifications as a man, except you need to choose a woman. Find a woman who is trustworthy and faithful in her walk with God—your pastor's wife, for example, or a woman minister, if they meet the criteria. Avoid the gossip or busybody.

It is never a good idea to talk about these issues with a person of the opposite sex unless it is a family member. Talking about sexual struggles with someone of the opposite sex opens a door of familiarity and can easily lead to making worse decisions than only looking at pornography.

In a nutshell, you want someone spiritual who will be gentle and understanding yet tough when needed.

Once you and your accountability partner have agreed to work together, it is vital that you be completely honest about your struggles with pornography. Discuss your failures and weaknesses. Try to pinpoint the stressors that feed your desire. The relief that comes from sharing this burden with a trusted friend is incredible, not to mention the euphoria from being liberated from this secret's heavy weight. You will no longer feel isolated in your battle, as you can talk openly about your struggles with porn. However, if you hide things from your accountability partner, you will experience more difficulty gaining spiritual ground.

As a word of caution, men, do not ask your wife to be your accountability partner. She will not understand you like another man will. A woman does not think like a man—God purposely created her different than you. Women do not know the pitfalls men face although they may be able to identify them. Your wife may see your mistakes as a marital issue instead of a personal struggle. The same applies to the ladies. Do not use your husband. You need an outside person who will not take your battle personally.

Men, at some point after seeking godly counsel, you will need to speak to your wife, but wait until your pastor, accountability partner, or both have given you the green light. Clearly, this will not be easy because men do not want their wives to perceive them as being weak. What begins your healing process will, undoubtedly, cause distress for your wife. Keeping your secret from her, however, is not an option. Understand that she may feel hurt, possibly angry. Give her time to work through the emotions, and give her room to be human. Encourage her to read this book or another book on this subject.

When my wife read *Every Man's Battle*, she saw that I was not abnormal. In fact, she realized the struggle men face in society with the constant bombardment of sexual imagery. Constant temptation is caused by immodest clothing, advertisements, and magazine covers at checkout stands, just to name a few. It confirmed to her that I wasn't just making up excuses for falling over these stumbling blocks.

Ladies, it is possible that you will face this as well when you have the talk with your husband about your porn struggle. His reaction may surprise you. He may take your fight personally. He may blow up in anger, feel rejected, or he could just act like it doesn't faze him. Be prepared for a confrontation or the cold shoulder.

Your accountability partner should have free access to your browser history on your computer and mobile device. Some filter/accountability software has a setting where an email is automatically sent to your accountability partner whenever you attempt to view inappropriate material or are online outside of your preset terms. They will have the authority to ask you at any time how you are doing. Be honest with your response! Your partner will pray with you and for you.

Your accountability partner will be available if you need immediate assistance should you be in a heavy onslaught of temptation, but it is important not to abuse this privilege. As discussed earlier, do not make provision for your flesh and then expect your accountability partner to bail you out. That person cannot do for you what you must do for yourself.

If you have been asked to be an accountability partner, understand the biblical instruction to the Galatians. Paul said, "Brethren, if a man is overtaken in any trespass, you who are spiritual restore such a one in a spirit of gentleness, considering yourself lest you also be tempted. Bear one another's burdens, and so fulfill the law of Christ" (Galatians 6:1–2).

Accountability partner, sharing someone's personal struggle with others will destroy your reputation and integrity and quite possibly the person you are helping.

The Bible says to restore others in the spirit of meekness. You must love this person through their struggle to get out of bondage. Never criticize, berate, or ridicule them. Keep their battle to yourself! It is no one else's business! Period! Confidentiality means you must keep it top secret. Sharing with others someone's personal struggle will destroy your reputation and integrity and quite possibly the person you are helping. Furthermore, if you are in a ministerial position within your church, you could open yourself and the church up for a lawsuit.

Accountability is a matter of trust. Trust is earned and learned. The one who is being accountable to you must learn to trust you. That will happen only when you earn it. Do not abuse or misuse the trust. It took a lot of courage for this person to come to you and ask for help.

The only reason to break this confidence is if you are obligated by the laws of your state to report specific crimes to law enforcement. These crimes usually include physical or sexual abuse of a child, neglect of a child, or child porn. Check the laws of your state to see who is obligated to report and for what reasons. The US Department of Health and Human Services website can be utilized for this purpose.[2]

When men who face these issues come to me, I always assure them that anything they say will remain confidential. If I think there could be the possibility of a legal matter, I warn them ahead of time of my obligation to report certain crimes. I want them to understand I am not going to break confidence unless legally obligated. If a child is involved in any way, I must protect those who cannot fend for themselves. These laws were established because protecting an innocent child is more important than protecting someone's confidence.

Here are some questions you should ask yourself. Be honest because dishonesty will not help you.

1. Have I prayed today?
2. Did I really pray?
3. Have I read or studied the Word of God?
4. Have I practiced quoting my verses?
5. Have I been in contact with my accountability partner?
6. Was I honest when speaking with my accountability partner?
7. What causes me to be tempted to view porn, or what are my triggers? (Some possibilities are flirtatious coworkers, suggestive music, or lingerie advertisements.)
8. When do I feel most vulnerable? (During or after a stressful time, being alone, after work, etc.)
9. Do I have an Internet filter and do I use it correctly? Did my accountability partner set the password?
10. What am I doing to combat this?
11. Am I making progress?
12. Do I feel negative or positive about my progress?
13. Do I attend church regularly?
14. Am I current on my tithes and offerings?
15. Are there other sin issues in my life that I am choosing to ignore?

Your accountability partner may ask you some of the same questions. You can certainly add more to the list.

Your accountability partner will

- pray with you and for you,
- check in with you frequently,
- check your online history on your computer and mobile devices,
- be available to help in times of need,
- encourage you in your battle.

ARMING YOURSELF FOR BATTLE

For though we walk in the flesh, we do not war according to the flesh. For the weapons of our warfare are not carnal but mighty in God for pulling down strongholds, casting down arguments and every high thing that exalts itself against the knowledge of God, bringing every thought into captivity to the obedience of Christ (II Corinthians 10:3–5).

Therefore submit to God. Resist the devil and he will flee from you (James 4:7).

If you have not figured it out by now, you are fighting for your soul. You must engage in this war if you want to be free from sin and have victory. Only you can fight your war. Other people can help, but responsibility for your own salvation lies in your hands (Philippians 2:12).

We live in a fleshly body that has a sinful nature. We struggle with our human nature, carnality, and sinful desires, and will until our time on this earth is over. We inherited a sinful nature at birth. But that does not mean we can blame God for making us that way. He did not plan for mankind to sin. Sin came about because of the disobedience of Adam and Eve.

Romans 3:23 says all have sinned. Conquering sin on our own is not possible. God can change us, however.

Romans 6:23 says the wages of sin result in death. Sin causes death, whether physical or spiritual. Before the fall in the Garden of Eden, death did not exist as part of God's plan for humanity. God intended for mankind to live forever. Sin resulted in an immediate spiritual death, or separation from God, and it brought about physical death. God had a plan in place should humanity fall. That plan included Jesus dying on Calvary, being buried in a tomb, and rising again (Revelation 13:8). He gives us the opportunity to regain the life that was lost because of sin.

The Bible gives instructions on how to deal with our fleshly nature. Through spiritual combat or warfare, we can overcome our carnal nature. We must fight against our physical desires and nature. We must also fight against the enemy of our soul.

If we fight our spiritual battles the correct way, victory is always guaranteed.

Warfare is never easy. When a country goes to war, winning is not definite. Success is not assured even with the best weapons, training, and sheer numbers of soldiers. But if we fight our spiritual battles the correct way, victory is always guaranteed.

The weapons of our warfare are not carnal. Man and corporations do not manufacture them. Therefore, God's weapons do not make sense to the carnal mind. They defy human thinking and logic. Our flesh says, "Prayer? That won't do anything. The Bible? What can that do?" Our weapons "do not wage war according to human standards" (II Corinthians 10:3 NET).

Our feeble brains cannot always comprehend the power of God's weapons. The weapons we have are mighty through God and are given to us for pulling down strongholds. A stronghold is a fortified position of the enemy, a military installation. If the enemy has built a fortress, only God's weapons have the ability to tear it down. If the enemy has set up base in our lives, such as some sin we just cannot seem to overcome, only God's weapons can destroy it.

His weapons cast down imaginations and high things that exalt themselves against God. The term "imagination" refers to human philosophies. The NET calls it "every arrogant obstacle that is raised up against the knowledge of God." So what are God's weapons? Ephesians 6 explains the pieces of armor and their use.

> Put on the full armor of God so that you can take your stand against the devil's schemes. For our struggle is not against flesh and blood, but against the rulers, against the authorities, against the powers of this dark world and against the spiritual forces of evil in the heavenly realms. Therefore put on the full armor of God, so that when the day of evil comes, you may be able to stand your ground, and after you have done everything, to stand. Stand firm then, with the belt of truth buckled around your waist, with the breastplate of righteousness in place, and with your feet fitted with the readiness that comes from the gospel of peace. In addition to all this, take up the shield of faith, with which you can extinguish all the flaming arrows of the evil one. Take the helmet of salvation and the sword of the Spirit, which is the word of God. And pray in the Spirit on all occasions with all kinds of prayers and requests. With this in mind, be alert and always keep on praying for all the saints (Ephesians 6:11–18, NIV).

First, Paul tells us to put on the whole armor of God, not just a part of it. We want to be completely protected from the enemy. It takes the entire suit of armor to be able to stand against the devil's schemes. Leaving some area exposed will cause us problems.

In Ephesian 6:12 Paul tells us we do not wrestle against flesh and blood. What does that mean? Our spiritual battle is not against other people. Our fight is "against evil rulers and authorities of the unseen world, against mighty powers in this dark world, and against evil spirits in the heavenly places." In other words, we wage war against Satan and his empire. We are not at war with each other. Our war is not against government. It is against the wickedness of Satan. This is a spiritual war.

Paul reiterates the importance of taking the whole armor of God. God's armor allows us to stand fast. We can resist the enemy, and when the battle is over we can stand resolutely on the solid Rock.

James 4:7 (KJV) instructs, "Submit yourselves therefore to God. Resist the devil, and he will flee from you." First, we must submit to God. Then by using the armor, we resist the devil and cause him to flee. Resistance does not just happen because we verbally say no. It occurs by engaging the enemy.

In Ephesians 6:14 Paul tells us to stand our ground and begins listing the armor. Physical armor protects various parts of the body. Each piece has a purpose and particular use. Each has a spiritual significance.

Belt of Truth

"Putting on the belt of truth." A belt covers the abdomen. Many vital organs occupy the abdomen: stomach, liver, kidneys, and spleen, among others. You do not want to get hit in the gut. This affects your courage. Have you ever had a "gut feeling" or made a gutsy move? If the devil can take away your courage, then you become fearful and afraid, which is one of the worst things that can happen. You will hesitate to fight; you will be afraid of failure and defeat. The devil wants you to be a "yellow belly chicken liver." If you are afraid of what may happen or show a lack of courage, you will surrender to the enemy.

Use the truth to overcome fear. Truth unlocks fear. Jesus said, "And you shall know the truth, and the truth shall make you free" (John 8:32, KJV). Why is that? Truth dispels Satan's lies. Truth speaks for itself. The Word of God needs no defense. It stands on its own merit. Charles Spurgeon said, "The Word of God is like a lion. You don't have to defend a lion. All you have to do is let the lion loose, and the lion will defend itself."[1]

> For God has not given us a spirit of fear, but
> of power and of love and of a sound mind
> (II Timothy 1:7).

Breastplate of Righteousness

A breastplate covers the heart and lungs. It protects your very life. Obviously, if you get shot in the heart, your chances of survival are very slim. The heart and lungs are vital for life. A shot to the chest usually results in death.

If the devil can take the life force out of you, you will not fight. He attempts to suffocate you with temptation. He will try to knock the wind out of you and take away your determination. You cannot fight spiritual battles if you are spiritually dead. That is the purpose of the breastplate of righteousness. Simply defined, righteousness is living right. Living correctly protects your vital organs.

You must protect your spiritual heart and lungs to stay lively. You must remain vibrant and full of God's joy, or you will not survive the battle. The joy of the Lord is your strength (Nehemiah 8:10). You must protect your vital organs by living right.

Footwear

Footwear? Battle armor? Shoes are just shoes, right? Decent footwear is often overlooked as important. Soldiers wear sturdy and rugged boots with their battle uniforms. Footwear serves various purposes. We wear boots in the winter to keep our feet dry from the snow, warm from the cold, and give us traction to be able to walk. No one likes wearing shoes that allow their feet to get wet in the rain. We do not want to slip and fall. Proper footwear also prevents blisters.

Military drill instructors and athletic coaches even teach the proper way to put on socks and shoes or boots. Legendary UCLA Basketball Coach John Wooden was known for his first lesson to new team members: how to put on your socks and shoes correctly. "The most important part of your equipment is your shoes and socks."[2]

Wooden's method of putting on socks prevented wrinkles that cause blisters. Athletic shoes are laced and tied in a way to keep the laces from coming loose, which causes shoes to slip. A football or basketball player is of little use to his team if he has blisters on his feet or his shoes frequently come off. A soldier with hurting feet will be a hindrance to his unit.

Spiritual footwear leads you to peace through the gospel. If you have no peace, you will worry. The result of the battle should always be peace. Whatever you do in this warfare, be consistently focused on what will bring peace. In a spiritual war, this will require total defeat of the devil because he will not allow peace as long as he is around. Keep your combat boots on in preparation for peace. The whole purpose of warfare is to gain peace.

If you slip or your feet are in bad health or the enemy knocks your feet out from under you, what happens? Down you go. Lying flat on your back renders you extremely vulnerable to the enemy. You may even drop your shield and sword. But if you get knocked down, it is important to get back up!

If you don't pay attention where you walk, you may trip over obstacles. Asaph stated, "But as for me, my feet had almost stumbled; my steps had nearly slipped. For I was envious of the boastful, when I saw the prosperity of the wicked" (Psalm 73:2–3). According to Proverbs 6:18, God hates feet that run to evil or mischief. Instead, we need to look to the Word of God. "Your word is a lamp to my feet and a light to my path" (Psalm 119:105). Wearing proper footwear and taking good care of your feet will help you walk in the right direction. The pursuit of peace is the right direction.

Shield of Faith

The shield of faith will stop the fiery darts of the enemy. The significance of the shield is that it is movable. It can be used to cover any vulnerable spot. If the enemy throws something at you, you can quickly and easily deflect the fiery dart with the shield.

What is faith? Faith is a belief, confidence, or certainty in something even without physical proof. The Bible says it is impossible to please God without faith. How can one come to God if they do not believe in Him? We exercise faith when we cannot see what is before us, and we must rely on God. We cannot watch our own back, but God can. We may not see a dart approaching, but God can. Our faith in God says, "No matter what, I know God will take me through. No matter what, God is in control. I do not know what tomorrow will bring, but God holds tomorrow in His hands."

The enemy will throw temptation at you from many directions. He will try drugs. He will try alcohol. He will attempt to frustrate you. He will try to get you to lie. If a particular lure doesn't work, he will move on to another temptation until he finds something that sticks. In many cases, it is pornography.

The enemy wants to destroy your faith. He throws things at you that may cause you to question God, to lose your faith and trust in God. You must keep the faith. Paul stated to Timothy, "I have fought a good fight. I have finished my course. I have kept the faith." You must keep faith alive. Faith says your vision will come to pass. Faith says God will heal you. Faith says God will supply the need. Faith states *you* may not be able, but God is. Faith says all things are possible with God. That includes victories over sin.

Helmet of Salvation

A helmet protects the head. A headshot usually kills. If the devil can get inside your head and warp your thinking, down you go. Far too many people have fallen to false doctrine and incorrect thinking. This was Satan's attempt to steal their salvation. But salvation comes from above. David said, "The Lord is my light and my salvation" (Psalm 27:1).

To have salvation, you must follow God's plan as spelled out in Acts 2:38. That is repentance, baptism in Jesus' name, and receiving the Holy Ghost. Salvation protects your mind. Having the Holy Ghost within straightens your thinking. It helps keep your mind clear and uncluttered. It helps you to see the things of God and, in turn, the things of the enemy. It helps you to hear the voice of God. It helps you to understand the things of God. Let's face it; it is not easy to comprehend the things of God without the Holy Ghost leading and guiding us. We must have the helmet of salvation to protect our minds.

Sword of the Spirit

Next, Paul lists the one and only offensive weapon. Prayer and fasting are not weapons, according to Scripture. Possibly one of the biggest reasons we struggle with sin comes from misunderstanding our offensive weapon. Paul did not negate the power of prayer and fasting. In fact, he said to pray always in the Spirit. The weapon, however, is the *sword* of the Spirit or the Word of God.

Satan does not care how much you fast and pray, what your name is, what church position you hold, the name of your pastor, or how much you give in the offering. He is not frightened by the fact that you go to church. As crazy as it sounds, he does not care whether you have been baptized in Jesus' name and have the Holy Ghost. That does not scare him at all.

If prayer and fasting were weapons, then how could Satan tempt Jesus immediately following Jesus' forty days of prayer and fasting? Satan should have been scared to death, but he wasn't. You might have noticed that it seems like your biggest temptations come right after fasting or time in prayer. If Satan was not frightened by Jesus' prayer and fasting, then ours certainly will not upset him.

If these things do not disturb or defeat Satan, what does? The sword of the Spirit, which is the Word of God. What a powerful weapon! It can stop the enemy in his tracks.

Jesus used Scripture to defeat each temptation from Satan. If you want to take the fight to the enemy, use the Word of God. If the enemy throws a temptation at you, use the Word of God to defeat him. We can see how to do that from the example Jesus gave. Do not use any random Scripture. Yes, the Bible is all truth. It requires truth to defeat Satan's lies. However, it takes truth that pertains to the lie he is throwing at you. Find scriptural passages that specifically target the temptation placed before you.

Here is a simple math equation to explain this concept: $1 + 1 = 2$.

Truth does not change. Truth is truth whether you believe it or not. You can try to explain that "two" is the wrong answer, and you may convince some people, but the correct answer to the above equation will always be "two." Someone's belief or opinion will not change the truth.

The Word of God and only the Word of God exposes Satan's lies.

The Word of God is truth (John 17:17). It has and will stand the test of time. The enemy of our soul will lie to us. Pornography will lie to us. We might even begin to believe the lies it tells. Yet the Word of God and only the Word of God exposes Satan's lies. Our argument is as empty as the enemy's if we do not refute his argument with truth.

> For the word of God is living and powerful, and sharper than any two-edged sword, piercing even to the division of soul and spirit, and of joints and marrow, and is a discerner of the thoughts and intents of the heart (Hebrews 4:12).

The Word of God is a powerful, sharp weapon. The Word of God is alive. It applies to every aspect of our lives. We must use it when resisting temptation.

So, what about prayer and fasting? Are they less important because they are not weapons? Quite the contrary. They are extremely vital. We will not survive without prayer and fasting. If they are not weapons, what are they? Prayer and fasting are the means of placing our lives on the altar as a living sacrifice (Romans 12:1). They cleanse us. They strengthen us. They are our exercise, our training, and our preparation. They connect us to Jesus. This is also why we need to go to church.

Think of prayer and fasting as going to the gym to work out. Exercise makes us energetic and fit, but right after a workout session, we feel weak. Our arms feel like spaghetti. Our legs are wobbly. We are winded and tired. We are out of energy and couldn't fight if we had to. If an enemy wanted to fight us this would be a superb time for him to pick a fight. A weapon of some kind could come in quite handy. However, the training pays off. The more training and exercise, the stronger we become.

When military recruits arrive at boot camp, they are immediately immersed into a regiment of physical training. They do pushups, pull-ups, and drills repeatedly. They learn to follow the commands of their drill instructor without question. This training exhausts them but also strengthens them. They learn how to use their weapons and how to care for them. They run for miles in full battle gear. Without proper exercise and training, they would be weak and sluggish and would not be able to endure prolonged battles.

Instructors have a reason for the repeated drills. They want the new soldiers to learn to act instinctively. When given a command, the soldier immediately obeys. Proper training and drills save lives. Boot camp is a safe environment to undergo basic training. Raw recruits are never sent straight to the battlefield.

Undergo proper training before you get to the battlefield.

The same applies to our spiritual man. We must spend time in prayer and fasting before the battle starts. We must continually study the Word of God. The psalmist said, "Your word I have hidden in my heart, that I might not sin against You" (Psalm 119:11). Memorize Scripture passages to use in battle. Use your weapon skillfully. Practice. Drill. Like soldiers, undergo proper training before you get to the battlefield.

When do you use the sword of the Scripture? Every time you are faced with temptation. If the verses are difficult to remember, write them out. You cannot allow temptation to catch you without your sword.

Get in the habit of wearing the complete set of armor. Know the proper use of your weapon. Keep yourself in good spiritual health. You cannot skip church and expect to be victorious. You need the protection of the body of Christ because the members watch each other's backs, which is the only area of the body not covered by armor.

When faced with temptation, bring that thought into captivity (II Corinthians 10:5), and run it through the Philippians 4:8 test.

> Finally, brethren, whatever things are true, whatever things are noble, whatever things are just, whatever things are pure, whatever things are lovely, whatever things are of good report, if there is any virtue and if there is anything praiseworthy—meditate on these things (Philippians 4:8).

Does the thought, idea, or temptation pass this test? If not, it needs to be discarded! Paul tells us in Philippians 4:9 to do what we have learned from him. Follow his example. Follow the principles he taught.

Through biblical instruction and the example of Jesus, we know our armor and weapons will work. We have everything we need to defeat the enemy and overcome our flesh. God has supplied us with the best munitions and protection, and they are guaranteed to work.

THE DREADED M WORD

All things are lawful for me, but all things are not helpful. All things are lawful for me, but I will not be brought under the power of any (I Corinthians 6:12).

Finally, brethren, whatever things are true, whatever things are noble, whatever things are just, whatever things are pure, whatever things are lovely, whatever things are of good report, if there is any virtue and if there is anything praiseworthy—meditate on these things (Philippians 4:8).

U h-oh, here we go. We are going to deal with the subject nobody wants to discuss; it is always hush-hush. Do we really need to talk about this? This is far more embarrassing than admitting you look at porn, right? What is the dreaded M word? Masturbation.

Most everyone knows what it is, and most everyone has done it at some point in his or her life. Just in case you are not familiar with the word, we'll define it. Masturbation is using one's hand to stimulate his or her genitals. If you made it through your teen years without doing this once, you are an extreme rarity. Many misconceptions, myths, and crazy ideas are believed about this topic, some funny and some not so funny.

Many have questions about this subject but are too uncomfortable to ask. Therefore, we need to discuss it. Many people feel condemned for masturbating and are confused by superficial or misguided teaching or a complete lack of instruction.

Unfortunately, the Bible does not mention the M word. It discusses many other sexual sins, but not once does it mention masturbation. I find that a little odd. Why would God's Word leave us without any definitive answers on this?

We cannot take the Bible's silence as condoning this behavior.

The Bible does not specifically mention many sins that we face, such as smoking, drug abuse, and pornography. Yet interpreting the Bible's silence on these things as condoning them would be dangerous. We cannot create our own ideas of what does or does not constitute sin. Instead, we must rely on godly principles to distinguish between right and wrong.

When it comes to masturbation, the physical act is not the only issue. The root of the problem is sexual desire or lust. The biggest sex organ is the brain. It is the control center for everything and is where the desire for sex begins. The body reacts to what happens inside the mind. If we are viewing or reading porn, our brain will activate the impulses, and masturbation follows. Thus, the first priority is that one needs to examine where his or her mind is.

Let's look at a key verse that explains this. Jesus said, "But I say to you that whoever looks at a woman to lust for her has already committed adultery with her in his heart" (Matthew 5:28).

For the sake of this discussion, let's consider the implication of Jesus' statement. The woman He referred to is not your wife; she is married to someone else. Just glancing at that woman is not a sin. It is when you let your eyes wander over her body and you begin to undress her in your mind. This initiates desire, and once you have lusted after her or desired to have sexual relations with her, it is the same as committing the act of sin. In other words, you committed adultery inside your mind. It is vital that you identify the point of when it goes from just looking to lusting. Once you reach that thin dividing line between looking and lusting, stopping the momentum is not likely to happen. One would do well to discipline the roving eye. If you glimpse someone you would consider attractive, train yourself to redirect your glance away from her. Don't engage the brain at all. It's the only sure cure.

With porn, it is all about lust and sex. Checking out the cute coworker and her figure, circling the block to get a better look at the attractive jogger, and watching porn can cause a man to desire the woman illicitly. For a woman, reading that steamy story or drooling over the buff jock will have the same result. The mind begins thinking about sex, and then it is "all systems go." Masturbation is then possible.

One simplistic way to consider the problem is guilt by association. The adultery or sin already has occurred in the mind. So masturbation in and of itself is not the main issue. It is what led up to it. The sin took place when the mind started having illicit sexual thoughts. If the mental act is sinful, then the physical act is too. Masturbation is a physical response to the sin committed in the mind. It is a very selfish, hedonistic act.

There are other implications as well as consequences for those who indulge in masturbation. Consider Onan, for example. Does the Bible say he sinned because he masturbated? No, it does not! Then what was his problem? Why did his actions displease God?

> And Judah took a wife for Er his firstborn,
> whose name was Tamar. And Er, Judah's first-
> born, was wicked in the sight of the Lord; and
> the Lord slew him. And Judah said unto Onan,
> Go in unto thy brother's wife, and marry her, and
> raise up seed to thy brother. And Onan knew that
> the seed should not be his; and it came to pass,
> when he went in unto his brother's wife, that he
> spilled it on the ground, lest that he should give
> seed to his brother. And the thing which he did
> displeased the Lord: wherefore he slew him also
> (Genesis 38:6–10, KJV).

The custom of the time later became part of the Mosaic Law. This law is spelled out in the New English Translation of Deuteronomy 25:5–10.

> If brothers live together and one of them dies
> without having a son, the dead man's wife must
> not remarry someone outside the family. Instead,
> her late husband's brother must go to her, mar-
> ry her, and perform the duty of a brother-in-law.
> Then the first son she bears will continue the
> name of the dead brother, thus preventing his
> name from being blotted out of Israel. But if the
> man does not want to marry his brother's wid-
> ow, then she must go to the elders at the gate
> and say, "My husband's brother refuses to pre-
> serve his brother's name in Israel; he is unwilling
> to perform the duty of a brother-in-law to me."
> Then the elders of his city must summon him
> and speak to him. If he persists, saying, "I don't
> want to marry her," then his sister-in-law must
> approach him in view of the elders, remove his
> sandal from his foot, and spit in his face. She

will then respond, "Thus may it be done to any man who does not maintain his brother's family line." His family name will be recorded in Israel as "the family of the one whose sandal was removed" (Deuteronomy 25:5–10).

Onan's brother, Er, died. Judah sent Onan in to have a child in his brother's stead so that Er would have a lineage. Onan did so, but he did not complete the act; he spilled his semen on the ground. For some reason, Onan did not want Er to have a lineage. Regardless of Onan's reason, his actions were selfish, disobedient, and evil. There was a provision should the man not want to marry his brother's widow (Deuteronomy 25), but Onan did not use that rule. This displeased God so He slew Onan.

Onan's actions have been misconstrued, and some even use the word "onanism" as a synonym for masturbation. However, Onan's sin was not masturbation; it was his refusal to impregnate his brother's wife. He refused to fulfill his obligation. His selfish actions are very similar to those of a porn consumer or a john using the services of a prostitute. He received sexual pleasure without giving of himself.

What Onan did leads to further questions. What about using a condom, birth control, or coitus interruptus? Onan was obligated to impregnate his deceased brother's wife in order to raise up children in his brother's name. By not fulfilling that obligation Onan committed an evil act. However, this example does not mean the Bible forbids having sexual relations with your spouse unless you plan to conceive a child; you can enjoy each other whenever you like. Neither does the Bible prohibit the use of birth control.

What if you masturbate so that you do not have to give yourself to your spouse? This behavior is wrong. We are not to defraud or deprive one another of our marital duties.

But because of immoralities, each man should have relations with his own wife and each woman with her own husband. A husband should give to his wife her sexual rights, and likewise a wife to her husband. It is not the wife who has the rights to her own body, but the husband. In the same way, it is not the husband who has the rights to his own body, but the wife. Do not deprive each other, except by mutual agreement for a specified time, so that you may devote yourselves to prayer. Then resume your relationship, so that Satan may not tempt you because of your lack of self-control (I Corinthians 7:2–5, NET).

In marriage, we give ourselves to our spouses. We become one flesh. God used Adam's rib to create Eve. She was literally part of him. Through marital relations, they joined again as one.

But from the beginning of the creation, God "made them male and female." "For this reason a man shall leave his father and mother and be joined to his wife, and the two shall become one flesh"; so then they are no longer two, but one flesh. Therefore what God has joined together, let not man separate (Mark 10:6–9).

Masturbation can cause one to deprive his or her spouse.

Each spouse has rights to the other spouse's body. The husband and wife fulfill each other. We are not to defraud, deprive, or abstain from sexual relations with our spouse except with mutual consent for a time of fasting and prayer. There is a reason for this. Satan will throw temptation at you to cause you to fail sexually. Masturbation can cause one to deprive his or her spouse.

God created the man to desire his wife and the woman to desire her husband. Dr. Juli Slattery makes this excellent observation: "A couple that has regular sexual intimacy can actually become addicted to each other."[1] Rather than being addicted to or hooked on porn and masturbation, enjoy the company of your spouse. The intimacy you gain with your spouse will be greater than any artificial partner.

This book is not intended to deal with every sexual problem known to humanity. If you are having sexual issues in your marriage, seek help. You need to talk to a professional, whether it is your pastor, a marriage counselor, or a medical doctor. Get the help you need.

Another aspect of masturbation that we must consider is this: Is it simply a habit? Some have said that men have a 72-hour sex cycle. According to the cycle, a man will feel the overwhelming need to have a sexual release every seventy-two hours due to the build-up of sperm in his body. While I cannot discount this entirely, I have not been able to find any scientific or medical proof of this cycle. What I can say is that if you have a habit of masturbation, psychologically you will feel the need for it.

The Book of Deuteronomy may shed light on this subject. "If one of your men is unclean because of a nocturnal emission, he is to go outside the camp and stay there. But as evening approaches he is to wash himself, and at sunset he may return to the camp" (Deuteronomy 23:10–11, NIV).

A nocturnal emission is the spontaneous release of semen that occurs during sleep, sometimes called a "wet dream." It most frequently happens during adolescent years. Semen can build up inside the male's body, and the body releases the stored semen naturally. I think if one often masturbates, more than likely there will be no nocturnal emissions. If God's Word mentions a nocturnal emission as a natural release, we can survive without masturbating.

Stop immediately and create a new, healthy habit to replace the bad one.

Unhealthy habits must be broken. It is not easy to train the body or mind to give up a habit, but it can be done. Stop immediately and create a new, healthy habit to replace the bad one.

> There is therefore now no condemnation to those who are in Christ Jesus, who do not walk according to the flesh, but according to the Spirit (Romans 8:1).

If you are feeling condemnation, remember it does not come from Jesus Christ. Condemnation is from the enemy who tells us we are going straight to Hell for our actions. Jesus is the only One who can condemn, yet He does not. What He does is convict. He gently nudges us and tells us we have sinned, and He is prepared to forgive when we are ready to repent. The important thing is, if we feel conviction for our actions, we must repent and not repeat them. We use the resources God has given to us to help us overcome the temptation. Remember we have choices. Make the right one. Run the desires and thoughts through the Philippians 4:8 test.

The issue with masturbation boils down to what caused the sexual arousal. If it is porn, a sexually explicit book, obscene song, flirty coworker, or anyone or anything other than your spouse, it is wrong. Any subsequent masturbation would also be wrong, but the issue was first raised in your mind.

John offered an example of this principle. "Anyone who hates his brother is a murderer, and you know that no murderer has eternal life in him" (I John 3:15, NIV). As hatred is a sin of the heart and in God's eyes the same as the physical act of murder, so is lusting after a woman the same as committing adultery.

If the mental act is sinful, the physical act is too. If one's mind is dwelling on sinful desires, sin has already been committed. Masturbation is simply a physical response to sin that is committed in the mind. I believe God cares more about the thoughts running through our mind than He does about the act of masturbation itself. If we get our mind in the right place, we can conquer the habit of masturbation.

Paul said he would not be brought under the power—be controlled—by anything. You must take the same tack as Paul and refuse to let anything control you. If masturbation has control of you, you must conquer it. Follow the biblical principles shared in this book. You can be victorious over all sinful, carnal habits and desires. Conquering masturbation is no harder than conquering pornography. The blood of Jesus is capable of cleansing all sin.

THE PROCESS OF RESTORATION

Restore to me the joy of Your salvation, and up-hold me by Your generous Spirit (Psalm 51:12).

Psalm 51 records David's prayer of repentance after committing adultery with Bathsheba and ordering the murder of her husband, Uriah.

> Have mercy upon me, O God, according to Your lovingkindness; according to the multitude of Your tender mercies, blot out my transgressions. Wash me thoroughly from my iniquity, and cleanse me from my sin. For I acknowledge my transgressions, and my sin is always before me. Against You, You only, have I sinned, and done this evil in Your sight—that You may be found just when You speak, and blameless when You judge. Behold, I was brought forth in iniquity, and in sin my mother conceived me. Behold, You desire truth in the inward parts, and in the hidden part

You will make me to know wisdom. Purge me with hyssop, and I shall be clean; wash me, and I shall be whiter than snow. Make me hear joy and gladness, that the bones You have broken may rejoice. Hide Your face from my sins, and blot out all my iniquities. Create in me a clean heart, O God, and renew a steadfast spirit within me. Do not cast me away from Your presence, and do not take Your Holy Spirit from me. Restore to me the joy of Your salvation, and uphold me by Your generous Spirit. Then I will teach transgressors Your ways, and sinners shall be converted to You. Deliver me from the guilt of bloodshed, O God, the God of my salvation, and my tongue shall sing aloud of Your righteousness. O Lord, open my lips, and my mouth shall show forth Your praise. For You do not desire sacrifice, or else I would give it; You do not delight in burnt offering. The sacrifices of God are a broken spirit, a broken and a contrite heart—these, O God, You will not despise. Do good in Your good pleasure to Zion; build the walls of Jerusalem. Then You shall be pleased with the sacrifices of righteousness, with burnt offering and whole burnt offering; then they shall offer bulls on Your altar (Psalm 51).

Only the blood of Jesus can wash away sin stain from our lives.

Proper repentance is necessary for overcoming sin. Only then can restoration happen. David acknowledged his sins before God. He then asked God to purge and wash him. Only the blood of Jesus can wash away sin stain from our lives. Then spiritual restoration can take place.

Restoration works in tandem with repentance. Once a person repents, the process of restoration begins. This process does not happen overnight—it takes time. Restoration occurs as we live a repented life and leave sin behind.

> I beseech you therefore, brethren, by the mercies of God, that you present your bodies a living sacrifice, holy, acceptable to God, which is your reasonable service. And do not be conformed to this world, but be transformed by the renewing of your mind, that you may prove what is that good and acceptable and perfect will of God (Romans 12:1–2).

According to this passage, we are to present our bodies to God. Yet we cannot offer a holy body on our own. Jesus became our mediator so that through Him we can become holy. Through repentance, we receive His mercy, forgiveness, and acceptance.

Repentance is a lifestyle and not just a prayer asking for forgiveness.

Romans 12:2 says that transformation comes from the renewing of the mind. Often we resort to praying for our weak flesh only after we have sinned or are spiritually worn out. However, prayer is something we need to do daily. We need to have a daily renewal of our minds before battle. Many people commit sin and then repent or ask God to forgive. Instead, we should live repented and prayed up so that we will not fall into sin. Repentance is a lifestyle and not just a prayer asking for forgiveness. In other words, our prayer life should be stable enough and consistent enough that we avoid falling into sin, rather than praying after we have fallen. Prayer is not supposed to be a last-ditch effort after all else has failed. When people place their spiritual lives in the proper priority, they live repented lives. Repentance is more than asking for forgiveness. It is living a life that is led by the Spirit of God.

> For if you live according to the flesh you will die;
> but if by the Spirit you put to death the deeds of
> the body, you will live (Romans 8:13).

Many Christians are guilty of running on empty by neglecting the spiritual aspect of their daily lives because they are too busy, or they quit trying because they have failed God so many times. Because of this, they are spiritually weak and drained. Many times when a person fails God, he or she may feel unworthy to pray or come back to church. It is the old "Oops, I messed up again" syndrome. Choose to do the right things. Never give up on God!

God is faithful to forgive if you ask. How many times will He forgive? Every time we sincerely ask. Repentance is not a one-time act that occurs only in the initial steps of salvation, that is, preceding baptism and being filled with the Holy Ghost. Repentance is a lifelong process. God not only forgives and restores us once, but He will do it again and again. His mercies "are new every morning" (Lamentations 3:23). He will continue to renew those who repent and whose faith and trust remain in Him.

David's prayer of repentance in Psalm 51:1 states, "Have mercy upon me, O God, according to Your lovingkindness; according to the multitude of Your tender mercies, blot out my transgressions. Wash me thoroughly from my iniquity, and cleanse me from my sin."

The love and grace of God cannot be comprehended. God forgave David of the heinous crimes he committed. If God could forgive David, He will forgive us. If God could forgive Paul of the atrocities he committed, He will forgive us.

Forgiveness is always available.

As Paul said in Romans 6, we strive to be dead to sin, but, thankfully, forgiveness of sins is always available. In fact, Paul implied that the saving potential is even greater after conversion.

> But God demonstrates His own love toward us, in that while we were still sinners, Christ died for us. Much more then, having now been justified by His blood, we shall be saved from wrath through Him. For if when we were enemies we were reconciled to God through the death of His Son, much more, having been reconciled, we shall be saved by His life (Romans 5:8–10).

We do not lose by giving God complete control of our lives. We do not lose if God gives victory. In view of God's provision of forgiveness, reconciliation, and armor for the battle, there is no excuse as to why we cannot be victorious.

We must learn to push stored images out of our minds by replacing them with Scripture. True, our memory of sin will never go away; however, we can bury them. Memories are like a landfill. After garbage is dumped in a landfill, it is covered with layers of dirt. A spoonful or two would not do the job. Layer after layer of soil is dumped on top of the garbage. Sometimes we think one prayer or one Bible verse will cover our memories. Then we are dumbfounded when the memory is still as vivid as it was before. It takes prayer and study and meditation on the Word of God to bury memories of sin. It is a long, drawn-out healing process. Living for God is a lifelong process of spiritual growth.

Once the memories are buried and God's Word is alive in our lives, we must never look back with a longing to return. Lot's wife could not bring herself to leave her beloved Sodom and Gomorrah. She was content to live in a place full of sin. God had something better for her, but she just had to have one more longing glance at the debauchery from which she was being delivered. God turned her into a pillar of salt as a reminder to all of us. Once He sets us free and restores us, we must not look back! Many of us have seen people's lives come to ruin because they could not leave their past sins buried.

After being trampled by the effects of sin, and receiving forgiveness of sins from Jesus, we must come to a place of restoration and renewal. Just being forgiven is not enough. We need to reclaim our "joy and gladness" as David requested in Psalm 51:8: "Make me hear joy and gladness, that the bones You have broken may rejoice."

Everyone likes a brand-new car. As a teenager, I wanted a 1988–89 Mustang GT convertible. I never got one and I can't purchase a new one now. However, getting a restored car is possible. I know a man who has a restored 1988 Mustang. It looks great, but it is not brand new. When God restores a person's spiritual life, He makes it better than new. He can give us joy, peace, love, happiness, and all kinds of good things in a way we have never experienced before.

Jesus Christ said, "The thief does not come except to steal, and to kill, and to destroy. I have come that they may have life, and that they may have it more abundantly" (John 10:10).

Live a repented life every day. That is having a more abundant life. That is how spiritual restoration works: living a life that is better than new.

INSTRUCTIONS FROM THE WISE MAN

Whoever gives heed to instruction prospers, and blessed is he who trusts in the LORD (Proverbs 16:20, NIV).

If you think you cannot fall into sexual sin, then you're godlier than David, stronger than Samson, and wiser than Solomon. – Bill Perkins[1]

I find it astonishing and extremely ironic that Solomon was so wise, and yet he did not control himself sexually. He had numerous wives and concubines. In its simplest form, a concubine is a woman who lives with a man for sexual purposes, but he is unable to marry her for some reason.

Having wisdom does not prevent us from making foolish mistakes if we do not apply it.

Solomon had so many women that it caused serious problems in his walk with God. Thankfully, he shared much of his wisdom with us so we can learn from his unwise mistakes. One of the most important lessons we can learn is that having wisdom does not prevent us from making foolish mistakes if we do not apply it. We need to take the Word of God and apply it to our lives daily.

Let's look at some of Solomon's writings on the subject of men, women, and his warnings to his son. In Proverbs 5–7, Solomon issues warnings against immoral women, prostitutes, and adulteresses. I must add that all this advice applies to pornography. Read these proverbs to learn the dangers:

Proverbs 5:1, 6:20, and 7:1 all tell a son to pay attention to, grasp, hold on to, and not let go of the commands of his father and mother. The parents are warning their son against the dangerous flirtatiousness and seduction of worldly women. Hear and heed the warnings, for nothing good will come of it!

The following verses come from the NIV.

Proverbs 5

3–8: For the lips of an adulteress drip honey, and her speech is smoother than oil; but in the end she is bitter as gall, sharp as a double-edged sword. Her feet go down to death; her steps lead straight to the grave. She gives no thought to the way of life; her paths are crooked, but she knows it not. Now then, my sons, listen to me; do not turn aside from what I say. Keep to a path far from her, do not go near the door of her house.

18–20: May your fountain be blessed, and may you rejoice in the wife of your youth. A loving doe, a graceful deer—may her breasts satisfy you always, may you ever be captivated by her love. Why be captivated, my son, by an adulteress? Why embrace the bosom of another man's wife?

23: He will die for lack of discipline, led astray by his own great folly.

Proverbs 6

23–29: The corrections of discipline are the way to life, keeping you from the immoral woman, from the smooth tongue of the wayward wife. Do not lust in your heart after her beauty or let her captivate you with her eyes, for the prostitute reduces you to a loaf of bread, and the adulteress preys upon your very life. Can a man scoop fire into his lap without his clothes being burned? Can a man walk on hot coals without his feet being scorched? So is he who sleeps with another man's wife; no one who touches her will go unpunished.

Proverbs 7

4–12: Say to wisdom, "You are my sister," and call understanding your kinsman; they will keep you from the adulteress, from the wayward wife with her seductive words. At the window of my house I looked out through the lattice. I saw among the simple, I noticed among the young men, a youth who lacked judgment. He was going down the street near her corner, walking along in the direction of her house at twilight, as the day was fading, as the dark of night set in. Then out came a woman to meet him, dressed like a prostitute and with crafty intent. (She is loud and defiant, her feet never stay at home; now in the street, now in the squares, at every corner she lurks.)

25–27: Do not let your heart turn to her ways or stray into her paths. Many are the victims she has brought down; her slain are a mighty throng. Her house is a highway to the grave, leading down to the chambers of death.

Solomon made it quite clear that the sexual advances of an immoral woman will cause many problems in a man's life. A man must not give in to the seduction, flirtation, and allurement of a female other than his wife. Pornography is seductive. It is alluring.

It is enticing. While a physical act of adultery is far more harmful than pornography, porn will ultimately lead to more serious problems. We cannot flirt with it. We cannot entertain thoughts of giving in. We must reject the temptation to give in.

In Proverbs 31:1–9, we find some much-needed warnings and instruction: "Give not thy strength unto women, nor thy ways to that which destroyeth kings" (Proverbs 31:3, KJV). The warnings of a parent should always be heeded. Here we see such a warning from a mother: "The first warning this mother gave was against moral impurity. She understood fully the weakness produced in a man who succumbs to immorality."[2]

Extramarital sex is one of the biggest temptations Satan has in his arsenal.

Sexual immorality has caused many great men to fall. We can look at numerous societal, governmental, and even religious leaders who have succumbed to the lure of sexual sin. As a child of God, we should not think for one moment that we are incapable of failing in this area because extramarital sex is one of the biggest temptations Satan has in his arsenal. I know of several ministers and their families who have been affected by sexual sins. Likewise, it is not uncommon anymore to hear of a married Christian woman finding new romance on some online forum.

We should never get to the point where we believe we are incapable of failing. There are far too many examples of respectable men and women who have succumbed to sexual temptation. Their reputations are ruined. Their integrity will always be questioned. They lost the respect they had worked so hard to gain. While they can be forgiven by God and saved, they will have great difficulty being trusted by others.

Solomon's instructions are from his personal experience. He had everything he wanted at his fingertips. If he saw a woman he wanted, he just added her to his harem. For men, this seems like a utopia, but listen to what Solomon had to say:

I also amassed silver and gold for myself, as well as valuable treasures taken from kingdoms and provinces. I acquired male singers and female singers for myself, as well as what gives man sensual delight—a harem of beautiful concubines. So I was more wealthy than all my predecessors in Jerusalem, yet I maintained my objectivity: I did not hold myself back from getting whatever I wanted, I did not deny myself anything that would bring me pleasure. So all my accomplishments gave me joy, this was my reward for all my effort. Yet when I reflected on everything I had accomplished and on all the effort that I had expended to accomplish it, I concluded: "All these achievements and possessions are ultimately profitless—like chasing the wind! There is nothing gained from them on earth (Ecclesiastes 2:8–11, NET).

Ecclesiastes 2:8 says Solomon had a harem of beautiful concubines that gave him sensual delight. Yet in verse 11 he stated that he gained nothing from these things; they did not satisfy. The NIV says, "Everything was meaningless." Porn says hedonism is the goal of life. Solomon lived that kind of lifestyle and realized how empty it truly was.

How could Solomon have any kind of meaningful relationship with so many women?

Solomon had an uncontrolled sexual appetite. He had seven hundred wives and three hundred concubines, and, if he wanted, could have intimate interludes with three different women a day. After that, he probably wouldn't see those same women again for another year. How could he develop any kind of meaningful relationship with these women? Would he even remember their names?

Consider another consequence of uninhibited sexual hunger: children. The Bible gives no indication as to how many children

Solomon had, but odds are he had many. Not only could he not have a meaningful relationship with his thousand wives or concubines, but he had so many children he could not maintain any kind of relationship with them either. What kind of father could he possibly have been?

The worst consequence of all is his lost relationship with God. Solomon not only had many foreign wives, which he had been instructed not to have, but he foolishly offered sacrifices to the gods of his wives. Solomon became idolatrous. Nehemiah said this of Solomon: "Nevertheless pagan women caused even him to sin" (Nehemiah 13:26).

Here are some other proverbs Solomon wrote.

O my son, give me your heart. May your eyes take delight in following my ways. A prostitute is a dangerous trap; a promiscuous woman is as dangerous as falling into a narrow well. She hides and waits like a robber, eager to make more men unfaithful (Proverbs 23:26–28, NLT).

He who covers his sins will not prosper, but whoever confesses and forsakes them will have mercy (Proverbs 28:13).

Like a city whose walls are broken down is a man who lacks self-control (Proverbs 25:28, NIV).

Why are consequences so quickly glossed over when moments of pleasure present themselves? Still, people give in to temptation all the time and forget the costs. We cannot live just for the moment.

We can learn both from Solomon's mistakes and from his wise instruction. He knew through sad experience that it is best to "live joyfully with the wife whom you love" (Ecclesiastes 9:9). Notice he said "wife" (singular, not plural). His example of uncontrolled lust and what it did to him should serve as a blaring warning to us. Sin has consequences attached that the temptation does not advertise. But righteous living has rewards that are known. Choose wisely!

HOW DO I TALK
TO MY CHILD?

Train up a child a child in the way he should go, and when he is old, he will not depart from it (Proverbs 22:6).

C onsider this mind-boggling statistic: the average age of first-time exposure to pornography is eleven. Some research suggests this could now be as low as eight. Due to easy access to the Internet, kids can see hardcore porn at the click of a mouse. A news story reported that "kids start watching porn from as early as the age of six."[1]

Today, Internet porn is hardcore, violent, and brutal.

Many children are just curious and sometimes innocently want to see a naked person, so they will initiate an Internet search. Maybe it is a pop-up ad that will lure them. Possibly a friend will show it to them. Whether or not they hunt for it, porn is hunting for them. Sadly, what they will see will not be basic softcore erotica. It is not the same porn I saw as a kid. I saw naked women in magazines and couples engaging in normal sex. Today, Internet porn goes to the extreme; it is hardcore, violent, and brutal. That is what kids will see. Being introduced to this kind of sexual activity at such a young age causes great damage to a developing brain. It will skew a child's view of the opposite sex, intimacy, and how to treat others.

Do not think for a moment that church kids are exempt from this. A large Oneness Apostolic church recently conducted a survey of sixty-one students, thirty-two boys and twenty-nine girls.[2] The results indicated the following:

Boys

94 percent have been exposed to porn. Only two boys said they had never seen it.

56 percent saw it again within six months after the first exposure.

25 percent see it weekly.

Girls

52 percent have been exposed to porn.

25 percent saw it again within six months after the first exposure.

7 percent see it weekly.

Combined

62 percent first saw porn on a mobile device, specifically an iPod Touch.

38 percent first saw it on a computer.

Ages of first-time exposure

9 percent sixteen or over

51 percent twelve to fifteen

24 percent nine to eleven

16 percent five to eight

We must wake up and realize this issue is not just among worldly children. Even church kids see porn, and some of them are hooked. Sometimes the exposure is accidental and sometimes it comes from a friend, but either result is just as disturbing.

A report by the National Coalition for the Protection of Children and Families states, "Young people growing up in our overly sexualized culture are being exposed to sexually explicit material on a daily basis through network television, movies, music and the Internet." The report added, "In addition, the majority of sex education is taking place in the media, not in the home, church, or school."[3]

Why do we leave this critical subject up to the schools to teach?

This brings us to the question, "What do I say to my child and when?" I'm often asked this question. In general, parents are uncomfortable with talking to their children about sex. Throw porn into the mix, and things get really awkward. Parents get cold sweats thinking about how to talk to their offspring about one of the most important aspects of life. Why is that? Why do we leave this critical subject up to the schools to teach? Why do we leave this up to society, their friends, television, movies, Internet, and worst of all, porn?

Parents, this is your job.

If you leave this up to the schools and society, what will they teach your kids? Christian values? Think again. Broad sexual acceptance is the norm outside the walls of the church. Homosexuality is no longer taboo. Transsexuality flaunts itself in the media. Gender identity issues are causing quite the stir. Don't leave these vital subjects to others. Parents, this is your job.

Gone are the days when we have "the talk"; by that time it is usually too late. Our son or daughter may already know far more than the basics. This child, your flesh and blood, needs to hear the truth and be taught wholesome values from you. If you do not instill these things into your children, someone else will fill that void and the information they get may not be morally correct. Your child's school will teach safe sex, may even hand out condoms, and yet never mention abstinence. Are those the values you want your child to have?

Talking to one's children about sex should not be so hard and uncomfortable. As mentioned previously, neither Solomon nor Paul tiptoed around sexual issues; they came right out and set firm biblical principles to live by. Why then do parents freeze up at the thought of discussing this subject with their children?

It is your duty as a parent to educate your child. Take your son or daughter to play catch or some other activity with just the two of you. After having fun for a while, sit down with them and begin to explain the truth about sex, boys, girls, and where babies come from. It might be best to have the same gender parent talking to the child. If that is not possible, step up to the plate. When do you start having these discussions and what is the appropriate age? Remember that by the age of six your child may have already seen porn.

The best time to start teaching your kids is when they begin to notice the differences between boys and girls. This usually happens around the age of four or so. They become aware of their bodies and may start asking questions. Keep the conversations age appropriate. When they ask where babies come from, tell them the truth without going into detail. Children need to understand there are differences between boys and girls, but they do not need graphic details. They need to learn modesty. They are not to show off their private parts nor view others' parts.

Respect your children enough to be honest with them during this stage, and they will respect you forever.

Do not fear talking to your preteen/early teen children. They want to be cool and knowledgeable, even if they have to pretend to know stuff so their friends won't think they are stupid or a "baby." In reality, they are confused. Adolescent hormones can put your child into a tailspin. Everything is new and different. Boys suddenly realize girls are cute. Girls suddenly notice the boys and vie for their attention. Remember when you were a young teen and all the strange things that were happening to your body? You may or may not have received adequate parental guidance, but don't leave your children without it. They need you to guide them through this stage. They will not ask outright. It is an incredibly awkward time of life for them. They need reliable and responsible parents to help them navigate safely. Respect your children enough to be honest with them during this stage, and they will respect you forever. They need to know they can ask you questions without fear.

You do not have to go into full detail, but you must be open and honest. Keep the dialog open for questions. Give your son or daughter a safe environment to talk to you. If you find out your child has seen porn or knows a little about sex, you may be upset, but never berate them. Instead, use this as a time to teach them where this path will lead. Reassure them that you want to help them and are always available and willing to talk. Let them know that your job as a parent is to help them, protect them, and raise them right. Resist the urge to be overbearing or you'll push them into hiding their struggles from you instead of confiding in you. Furthermore, exchanges such as these cannot be a one-time conversation. You need to check up on your son or daughter on occasion. They need to learn self-control and discipline, and their best teacher is your example.

Herman Gantt spoke at a youth rally. During his message, he mentioned issues that came up with his own children, like wanting to do something he would not allow. They asked if he didn't trust them. He said, "I trust you; I just don't trust your hormones."

Let's discuss electronic media devices and the snares they present. A smartphone is capable of accessing the Internet. There are ways to prevent children from getting open access to everything the Net has to offer. Each device is different, but it will have an area that allows the parent/guardian to set restrictions on what the device can and cannot do. For example, I set my kids' phone restrictions so they will not allow the standard browser to operate. Instead, I loaded a browser app that automatically filters web content according to the level I have set. I also turned off their ability to load apps from the app store. They must come to me if they want to load a new app.

Many apps are dangerous. For example, Snapchat allows a person to take a photo and send it to someone else who has this app. The app will delete the photo ten seconds after the other person has opened it on their device. Many believe this app is safe since it removes them automatically. However, as some have found out, a person can save the picture to their device's photo file before the app removes it. This is dangerous because some have sent explicit photos thinking they are safe only to find out the pictures have been saved, and in some cases posted on the Internet.

Sexting is an enormous problem among teens. It is time for a little education for the naive among us. A sext is sending or receiving a sexually suggestive text or email often accompanied with a nude or nearly nude photo or video. The statistics are overwhelming. In 2009, Cox Communications published the results of a survey of teens ages thirteen to eighteen. Of this group, 17 percent had received a sext and 9 percent had sent one. The majority of teens think sending sexts of someone under eighteen is wrong. The top reason for a teen to send a sext is because someone asked him or her to do it (43 percent).[4] Headlines scream of school students sending nude photos and sext messages to each other.

A nude photo of a child under the age of eighteen is by definition child pornography. These photos often end up being shared among peer groups and may end up online. Sexual predators have been known to entice youths into sending nude pictures and, even worse, meeting face to face. It is increasingly common to hear of teachers soliciting or sexting students, or worse.

Consider the many leaked nude snapshots of celebrities. Unfortunately, once a nude picture is in cyberspace, it never goes away. A young teen may not understand the consequences of sharing a nude or nearly nude photo.

As new apps are developed, it is imperative that parents pay attention to what the app does and how it operates. You may not be the most tech-savvy person, but that does not excuse you from being aware of modern technology. If you are not sure what to do, ask a youth pastor, an older, responsible teen in your church, or do an Internet search on dangerous apps for kids, but certainly pay attention. Parents, please understand that today's society is far different than when most of us grew up. Thankfully, statistics indicate when parents are actively involved in raising their children and paying attention to these kinds of issues, children are much less likely to get caught up in these dangerous behaviors.

Just as Jesus is patient and longsuffering with us, we need to be patient and longsuffering with our kids. We need to follow His example. We should show our children we love them in spite of their mistakes and issues. Much like our accountability partner, we must earn the trust of our children. Open communication is a must. We need to be engaged in our children's lives. They may not say it, but they appreciate it.

THE WATCHMAN ON THE WALL

Son of man, I have appointed you a watchman. . . . If I say to the wicked, 'You will certainly die,' and you do not warn him to turn from his evil conduct so that he may live—that wicked person will die for his iniquity, but I will hold you accountable for his death. But if you warn the wicked and he does not turn from his wickedness or from his evil conduct, he will die for his iniquity and you will have saved your own life (Ezekiel 3:17–19, NET).

Dear Pastor,
    I have been a faithful member of your church for many years now, and not one time have I heard you speak on the issue I face in my life. I don't come to you for help because I feel ashamed and scared. If I only knew you cared enough about this to deal with it. Please tell me how to get free from pornography!
    Signed,
    Anonymous

We are to teach the truth. All of it.

I never wrote a letter like the above, but like so many who have struggled with pornography, I sure wanted to because it is such a taboo subject in our "Puritan" church culture. On the other hand, society openly accepts pornography as mainstream. The world sees nothing wrong with discussing sexual sins and in fact promotes sin and shoves it in our faces. However, the church is strangely silent on what a person must do to get free and stay free from pornography. In the Old Testament, Mosaic law prohibited all manner of sexual sins, and Solomon sounded numerous warnings about the seduction and allurement of sexual sins. In the New Testament, Paul dealt with sexual wickedness when writing to the Corinthian church. The Bible did it; why don't we? Don't we know we are to teach the truth? All of it? The truth includes more than the gospel and the Acts 2:38 message. The entire Bible is truth.

For those of you brave enough to deal with this issue, I thank you. So do the men and women who struggle in this area, even if they do not thank you personally. While the conflict is different for men and women, both face it in some manner. Pornography has ensnared numerous men and women.

Pastor, if you have never discussed this issue in your church, it is most likely for one of these four reasons:

1. *You are naïve to the problem.* For whatever reason, you have no clue these sins have infiltrated your church. You know they are sinful, but think they could never touch the members of your church. The reality is you have your head in the sand.

I say this because one pastor told me porn was not a problem in his church. I could not believe my ears. I didn't know whether to laugh or yell at him. I wanted to tell him, "Give me fifteen minutes with your men, and I'll find several who do."

Don't be naïve. The truth is pornography binds men and women in our churches. They want help, but they are trapped. Your silence is deafening. Be courageous and confront this issue.

2. *You know this is an issue, but you ignore it because you do not know how to deal with it.* You are unsure what to say. You may be afraid of it. It is taboo. You do not know how people will accept your confrontation.

Maybe you honestly have no idea how to approach the subject. You may recognize the urgent need, but what do you say? I'll tell you. Start with the basics. Have split sessions for men and women. Then open up: you talk to the men while your wife talks with the women. If you still feel inadequate, contact someone who has dealt with this and ask for guidance. Trust me, those who are bound by this will thank you. This is a moment you as a pastor will gain a real connection with the men in your church. You will earn their respect. The same relationship will happen between your wife and the ladies. I know this from experience.

Stiffen your backbone and confront this sin. Be kind to those who are bound. They do want help and are tired of feeling condemnation. Don't add to that. Be a helping hand instead of one who rejects or ignores the sinner.

3. *You struggle with pornography yourself.* If you battle with porn yourself, it makes the subject tough to discuss. How do you tell others how to be free from sin if you cannot seem to get there yourself? Get help! I do not suggest you open up to the men in your church about your personal struggle. Bring in a guest speaker to teach on it. You will learn something yourself. Whom do you bring in? Find someone you know who has overcome this very issue. Invite a minister who has taught on this. There are plenty of qualified men who can.

4. *The worst reason of all: You know it is an issue, yet you refuse to discuss it.* Some pastors may avoid the topic because sex is highly personal. "We don't talk about those things in our church." It is like telling those who struggle, "Sorry, but you are on your own. The church will not help you." It is easier to remain silent than to be real and talk openly about it. The problem with remaining silent is that those who need help never get it!

Think of the priest and Levite who both saw the man who had been robbed, beaten, and left naked and half dead on the side of the road. He was in desperate need of help. Those who should have helped refused. The situation was too messy. They would defile themselves. They were too busy. They had more important things to do. They could not be bothered. Thankfully, a Samaritan saw the man and helped him. Imagine needing immediate medical care and having a paramedic glance at you and then ignore you.

If we are not careful, we can act the same as the priest and the Levite and the uncaring EMT. We may think, "I do not have time to help a dirty, filthy sinner who surely knows better than to have gotten himself in that kind of situation." But we should be careful; we are displaying condemnation, which will cause further harm to those who long to be free and are in need of our help. We should not leave our duty to some cast-off like the Samaritan.

I used to listen to a well-known radio psychologist. When a woman asked for help in dealing with her husband's porn addiction, the psychologist ridiculed the man for exhibiting a character flaw in his life. She may have been a professional, but she had no idea how this problem affected men. Certainly, not all men hooked on porn see it as a problem. But for those who do and who want help, how can passing judgment on their character help?

Not long after this, some nude photos of the psychologist were leaked onto the Internet. For me, knowing she had posed for a boyfriend in her younger years made her self-righteous, judgmental attitude toward the addicted man all the worse. I could no longer listen to her program.

We should never turn up our nose at a sinner. Did Jesus look down on the harlot brought before Him? No. He who was without sin told her that He did not condemn her (John 8:3–11). In fact, Jesus did not turn away any sinner who came to Him for help or deliverance.

Is it pleasant to deal with pornography? Absolutely not. However, don't sweep it under the rug just because it is an awkward subject. Do not disregard or ignore it. Instead, heed the warning of Ezekiel.

In today's society, with such easy access to pornography, someone in your church is bound by it.

Pastor, you are the watchman on the wall. Your role is to lead others to Jesus and teach them how to overcome sin. Pastors do an enormous disservice when they avoid confrontations of distasteful and frightening subjects. Please understand: someone in your church is bound to be ensnared by various sexual sins, considering today's easy electronic access to pornography. Mark it down.

Let me give you some eye-opening realities. In 2014, I conducted a survey of Oneness men at an Apostolic men's conference. I will not give the name of the church since this could easily be any church. The men had all been baptized in Jesus' name and filled with the Holy Ghost. Here is the result:

- 100 percent stated they had seen pornography.
- 100 percent indicated pornography had tempted them.
- 13.3 percent said pornography currently bound them.
- The average age of first-time exposure to pornography was 11.6 years.
- 40 percent had struggled with porn for over ten years.
- 46 percent currently did not have an accountability partner.

Of those who stated they were no longer addicted, but still struggling:

- 16.6 percent viewed porn two or three times a month.
- 8.3 percent viewed porn weekly.
- 33.3 percent viewed porn several times a week.
- 41.6 percent viewed it daily.

These findings translate to 83 percent of these men habitually viewing porn once a week or more. Only 20 percent ever sought help from their pastor. Why? Could it be that we pastors have not given our guys the reassurance they can come to us for help in this area?

I also conducted a voluntary questionnaire among ministers. Due to the fact it was voluntary, only a small amount completed the survey. However, the information gathered indicates many in ministry struggle with porn or have struggled in the past. I cannot possibly give an exact percentage of ministers who deal with this without being able to conduct a controlled study. However, a 2001 report from *Leadership Journal* indicated 51 percent of pastors say Internet pornography is a possible temptation, while 37 percent admit it is a current struggle.[1]

What about the women who deal with this? While I have not conducted a survey of women, statistics from other Christian organizations indicate that up to 30 percent of Christian women view pornography regularly. While these statistics are for Christian women in general, it is safe to say there are Oneness Apostolic women who have been trapped by pornography. The percentage is not crucial; one person is one too many.

Pornography also affects many ministers and their families. If your family is under attack, odds are even higher that those under your care are too. Gone are the days where we can just assume men and women know that pornography should be avoided. They do know it! But just knowing something is unhealthy is not enough to help them if they struggle. We must confront the issue of pornography and all the problems associated with it. More important, we must give biblical instruction on how to get free from it.

We must take off the blinders and face reality. Pornography is quite likely the most common sin among men in your church, since statistics seem to prove it. Watchman, please address pornography for the sake of those in your congregation that are bound! I am begging you, from one who sat on a church pew and was bound by pornography for many years of my life.

One day, I received a one-word email from a man who struggled with this. It said, "Help!" Man of God, hear the cry for help and let it stir you with compassion.

DIRECTIONS AND TIPS

This Book of the Law shall not depart from your mouth, but you shall meditate in it day and night, that you may observe to do according to all that is written in it. For then you will make your way prosperous, and then you will have good success (Joshua 1:8).

Therefore, brethren, be even more diligent to make your call and election sure, for if you do these things you will never stumble (II Peter 1:10).

Success means different things to different people. Some think it means to achieve a particular goal, reach a certain status in life, conquer a habit, or learn to play an instrument. For others, it is to graduate from school, be the best at something, have a plush bank account, or win a championship. Being respected is one way we define success; conversely, the lack of respect is one of our biggest insecurities. In addition, we often measure our success by comparing it with the success of others. Each of us has our own idea of what success means.

If we are not careful, we may see conquering our porn habit as the ultimate achievement and, therefore, it would be our greatest success. In one sense, it is true that would be successful. However, God's view of success is something far different than ours. We need to discover His idea of success so we do not sell ourselves short.

Joshua 1:8 uses the word "success." This is the only place in the King James Version of the Bible you will find that word. The concept of success is found in many places, but here the actual word is used. Joshua stated that if a person did the three following things they would prosper and have not just success but *good* success: (1) keep God's word continually in their mouth, (2) meditate on it day and night, and (3) do all that is written in it.

Therefore, to God success means living right in every area of our lives. We obey Joshua 1:8 when we learn the Word of God, study it, and apply it to our lives. This takes a concerted and focused effort. The Bible does not say this fight will be easy, but it does guarantee spiritual success if we fight the correct way.

We live in a day and age where Satan is attacking relentlessly. His objective is to divert our attention off of godly success and onto man's idea of success. The psalmist Asaph confessed, "But as for me, my feet were almost gone; my steps had well nigh slipped. For I was envious at the foolish, when I saw the prosperity of the wicked" (Psalm 73:2–3, KJV).

If your mind is not made up, you will fail! Asaph nearly slipped because his eyes had wandered to the wrong place, but he had his mind made up. A paraphrase of his words would be, "I almost fell, but I didn't lose it because but I had a made-up mind. I faced a weak moment, a time of uncertainty, but I did the right thing." You must have a made-up mind! Get a determination burning in your gut to fight this out and win the war! If you have more confidence in your enemy's ability than in your own, you will lose your battle. However, if you have assurance in God, you will gain the victory. "Greater is he that is in you, than he that is in the world" (I John 4:4, KJV).

Pornography (including romance novels) and other sexual enticements are fantasyland. They distract. They make us dream of, wish for, and desire things that appear glamorous and exciting. Just remember the world's idea of success is not the same as God's view of success. Temptation is deceptive. Jesus is truth.

Here are some inspirational directions and tips.

This war is worth fighting.

Think of the rewards for overcoming pornography. Freedom from porn will make you a better spouse. You will feel better about yourself. Also, Heaven will be worth the effort! Don't just live for the here and now. Live for a future eternity with Jesus! Heaven will make the frustrations we go through and battles we wage all worthwhile.

Identify your triggers.

What things cause you to want to view porn? In other words, what ignites the spark? It might be an attractive or flirty co-worker or a cute neighbor. Maybe it is an adverse state of mind such as frustration, stress, anxiety, boredom, or loneliness. Holidays can be challenging and could easily cause an issue. Other triggers could be a cloudy, foggy mind due to illness or other condition. Maybe you have multiple triggers. You need to learn what they are and then prepare to fight when that temptation presents itself.

Check in with your accountability partner.

An accountability partner is a vital tool in this battle. Read the chapter dealing with this subject again.

If you fall, get up!

Don't wallow in the mud. Don't beat yourself up. Turn your mistake into a learning moment. A failure can become a victory if you learn from it. Then make sure you do not repeat the error.

Safety industries teach how to avoid slips, trips, and falls. How does a person prevent a fall? Refrain from risky situations. Be aware of your surroundings. Pay attention to what you are doing. Don't allow yourself to be distracted. Wear proper footwear. Watch out for obstacles and hazards. These same rules apply to our spiritual walk. Be aware of your spiritual surroundings and climate. The Word of God is a lamp to our feet and a light to our path (Psalm 119:105). Using His Word will prevent slips, trips, and falls.

Don't put undue pressure on yourself.

Do not pressure yourself into being "perfect." While living totally sin free is our goal, understand we still live in a body of flesh that will never be perfect in this life. We will achieve perfection only when we make it to Heaven. Instead of aiming for something that is unattainable in a corruptible body, set goals that can be reached. When you meet these objectives, set new goals.

Stop cold turkey if at all possible!

The best thing is to attempt to stop immediately—cold turkey. Cease and desist! Set a thirty-day goal of not viewing porn at all. Check off each successful day on a calendar. You will find this is easier to do than you think. If you mess up, start over. After thirty consecutive days, you will realize the accomplishment, and you'll be able to use that as a springboard.

If thirty days seems too daunting or is simply not working, try a different method. Let's say you want to paint the interior of your house. That is the ultimate goal. You will not achieve that goal until you paint all the rooms. You won't paint all the rooms until you paint the walls in the first room. Start with one wall. Then paint the next. Complete one room before moving to the next room. Once all the rooms are finished, move to the hallways. When you have achieved each of the smaller goals, you will discover you have succeeded in meeting your original objective of painting the entire house.

Set goals that match your level of porn habit. If you have a daily habit, set a goal of going a week without porn. When you meet that goal, set a new one for two weeks. Then establish a new objective for a full month, and so on. Build on the momentum you are gaining. But I caution you not to reward yourself with a porn session! That will defeat your purpose.

Smaller goals are easier to reach and give you the sense of accomplishment and positive reinforcement. With attainable goals, you will not feel as if the world has caved in on you if you mess up, and it is much easier to get up and try again.

This is not the same as weaning off of porn. Watching fifteen minutes instead of an hour is not victory. You will not have success by weaning. You cannot wean off of sin. You either sin or you do not sin. To wean yourself is to make provisions for your flesh. Be prepared for withdrawal symptoms.

Keep a personal journal.

Make entries for each time you struggle and fall. Be sure to include what you did to recover and get back on your spiritual feet. Add entries when you defeated temptation, including what you did to overcome the enticement. Write down passages of Scripture that give you strength. Also, write down any thoughts God gives you and any messages taught or preached by your pastor that give you direction.

In time, you will notice that positive entries about progress and victories are beginning to outnumber negative, down-in-the-dumps entries like "I messed up." Review the helpful entries when you face difficulties.

Change your daily routine.

We are creatures of habit. We go through the same motions every day. We get up, get dressed, use the restroom, and then head to the kitchen for coffee. Every single day. The rest of the day is full of repetition as well. Unfortunately for many, porn is part of that routine. It is time to mess up the daily schedule. Make sure to include prayer and Bible reading early in the day. When it is time for your porn "appointment," do something else. Read your Bible. Pray. Fill that time with something encouraging and productive. Don't replace porn with a different sin or weight. For example—watching TV, movies, or trolling Facebook all day. That will not help you. You have given that time to indulge your flesh long enough. Use it to strengthen your spiritual man.

Be smart with your computer and devices.

Place your computer in a well-traveled area of the house where you will not be able to hide what you are looking at from passersby. Also, use a filter. You should have your accountability partner or spouse set the password so you cannot turn the filter off on a whim.

Memorize the Word of God.

Keep notecards handy with the weaponized verses you have chosen to use when tempted. You need to memorize these verses, but keep the cards ready in case you suffer a mental lapse. Place them in various locations—in your car, on the bathroom mirror, in your wallet, on the refrigerator, on your computer, and wherever else you deem helpful.

Get into the habit of memorizing positive and uplifting verses in addition to your weaponized verses. It is easy to do. Start with Psalm 1. The more Word you have in you, the stronger you become. Remember Psalm 119:11, "Your word I have hidden in my heart, that I might not sin against You."

Learn the art of averting your eyes.

Do not lust after her beauty in your heart, nor let her allure you with her eyelids (Proverbs 6:25).

Job stated, "I made a covenant with my eyes not to look lustfully at a girl" (Job 31:1). It is a challenge to avert your eyes away from something that is attracting your attention. However, we must learn to look away from anything that plants improper sexual thoughts in our minds. This is best accomplished through consistent practice and quoting verses that combat the temptation. Don't ogle the woman who is wearing next to nothing. Look elsewhere and quote, quote, quote those verses. It takes self-discipline. We must make the right choices if we hope to gain victory.

Get active in the church.

Men, get actively involved in the men's ministry of your church. Ladies, get actively involved in the women's ministry. Discuss this topic during those meetings. You will find others who have dealt with this in their lives and will gain strength and support from their experiences.

Do not neglect prayer, fasting, and church attendance.

Jesus Christ died on Calvary to give us the opportunity to have everlasting life. We can enjoy that only when we live for Him. We must make up our minds that we are going to live for God no matter what. We must have the determination to persevere.

We must live right, act right, talk right, walk right, think right, and do what is right. Thankfully, He gives us all the resources we need to help us do just that.

Jesus loves you in spite of your sin, in spite of what you have done or where you have been. His blood was shed on Calvary for you! It is His desire to set you free as well. That is why He did the hard part.

Simply put, recognize or admit your problem and then repent. Get an accountability partner. Memorize Scripture passages to quote when tempted. Remove weights and hindrances from your home and life. Use all the available tools you can. Stay confident and focused on victory! And never quit!

You can do this! How do I know? Jesus delivered me from a daily porn habit. Let me tell you, being on this side of the battle is so refreshing. I want to encourage you today to look upward. Look up to your Savior and not downward to the pit. Get focused on the outstretched hand that is there to pull you out.

You can escape through the love of Jesus.

> For the LORD is good; His mercy is everlasting, and His truth endures to all generations (Psalm 100:5).

NOTES

Chapter 5

[1] "Pornography." By permission from *Merriam-Webster's Collegiate Dictionary, 11th Edition* © 2016 by Merriam-Webster, Inc.

[2] Ibid.

[3] Ibid. "Fornication."

[4] Thayer's Greek Definitions, rev 14.

[5] πορνεία – porneía (From porneuó): fornication πορνεύω - porneuó (From porné): to commit fornication πόρνη - porné: harlot, whore πόρνος - pornos: a fornicator, whoremonger ἐκπορνεύω - ekporneuó: give self over to fornication *Strong's Exhaustive Concordance of the Bible, King James Version*, Abingdon edition 1984.

[6] Porneia (the root of the English terms "pornography, pornographic"; cf. */pórnos*) which is derived from *pernaō*, "to sell off") – properly, a *selling off* (surrendering) of sexual purity; *promiscuity* of any (every) type. *The Discovery Bible New Testament, HELPS Word-studies*, Gary Hill, 2011.

[7] "Prostitution." *Merriam-Webster.*

[8] Jennifer Ketcham, "Why Would Montana Fishburne Become a Porn Star?" *The Huffington Post*, August 11, 2010.

[9] Ray Nothstine, "Cosmopolitan Magazine Lands on Sexual Exploitation 'Dirty Dozen' List; Pushes BDSM Sex on Underage Girls." *The Christian Post*, September 18, 2015, www.christianpost.com/news/cosmopolitan-magazine-lands-on-sexual-exploitation-dirty-dozen-list-pushes-bdsm-sex-on-underage-girls-145583.

Chapter 6

[1] Thomas Politzer, "Introduction to Vision & Brain Injury," https://nora.cc/for-patients-mainmenu-34/vision-a-brain-injury-mainmenu-64.html.

[2] Juli Slattery, "Barriers and Baggage," *Thriving Family*, Oct.–Nov. 2015, 28.

[3] Julia Hislop, "Female Sex Offenders Are Often Overlooked," *The New York Times*, February 21, 2013, www.nytimes.com/room-

fordebate/2013/02/20/too-many-restrictions-on-sex-offenders-or-too-few/female-sex-offenders-are-often-overlooked.

[4] "Cyber-porn held responsible for increase in sex addiction," *The Washington Times*, January 26, 2000, www.washingtontimes.com/news/2000/jan/26/20000126-010843-1665r/.

[5] Robert Weiss, "Understanding Sex Addiction in the New Media Frontier," Robert Weiss MSW, www.robertweissmsw.com/sex-addiction/page/2/.

[6] Sam Black, "Your Brain's Sexual Cocktail," *The Porn Circuit*, Owosso, Michigan: Covenant Eyes, Inc., 2013.

[7] Gene McConnell, "Toxic Porn, Toxic Sex: A Real Look at Pornography," www.everystudent.com/wires/toxic.html.

[8] James Dobson, "Fatal Addiction: Ted Bundy's Final Interview," Florida State Prison, January 23, 1989, Transcript: www.pureintimacy.org/f/fatal-addiction-ted-bundys-final-interview.

[9] "Habits and Demographics," *Pornography Statistics*, Owosso, Michigan: Covenant Eyes, Inc., 2013.

[10] E. L. James, www.eljamesauthor.com/books/fifty-shades-of-grey.

[11] Top Ten Reviews. "Internet Pornography Statistics Overview," www.Internet-filter-review.toptenreviews.com/Internet-pornography-statistics-overview.html.

[12] "Dirty Girls Ministries," www.dirtygirlsministries.com/dgcc/. "Prostitution." Merriam-Webster.

Chapter 7

[1] "Interview Adam Glasser," *American Porn*, PBS Frontline, 2002, Web Transcript.

[2] Tyler Kingkade, "Straight Men Who Watch More Porn Are More Supportive of Same-Sex Marriage: Research," *The Huffington Post*, May 2, 2013, http://www.huffingtonpost.com/2013/02/05/porn-same-sex-marriage_n_2624268.html.

Chapter 8

[1] Steven Hirsch quoted by Ralph Frammolino and P. J. Huffs-tutter, "The Actress, the Producer and their Porn Revolution," *Los Angeles Times*, January 6, 2002.

[2] "The Purpose of Women, AntiPorn Resource Center, www.oneangrygirl.net/antiqoute24.htm.

[3] Shelley Lubben, *Truth Behind the Fantasy of Porn*, Shelley Lubben Communications, 2010, 4–5.

[4] "The Secret History of the Other Hollywood," CourtTV.com, July 23, 2001, web.archive.org/web/20010727183606/http://www.courttv.com/talk/chat_transcripts/2001/0723mitchell.html.

[5] Martin Amis, "A Rough Trade," The Guardian, March 15, 2001 (Web address withheld due to graphic content).

[6] Jonathon E. Fielding, "Adult Film Industry," County of Los Angeles Public Health, September 17, 2009, file.lacounty.gov/bc/q3_2009/cms1_137588.pdf.

[7] Kathleen Miles, "LA Porn Stars Have More STDs Than Nevada Prostitutes, Study Says," *The Huffington Post*, November 1, 2012, www.huffingtonpost.com/2012/11/01/la-porn-stars-stds-nevada-prostitutes-study-video_n_2058406.html.

[8] Amis.

[9] Tim Marchman, "Filmed Assault? Tim Marchman Talks to Regan Starr," *New Partisan*, N.p., 1 May 2004, www.newpartisan.squarespace.com/home/filmed-assault-tim-marchman-talks-to-regan-starr.html.

[10] "10 Ex-Porn Stars Share Their Most Disturbing Stories from Within the Industry," Fight the New Drug, April 26, 2015, www.fightthenewdrug.org/10-porn-stars-speak-openly-about-their-most-popular-scenes.

[11] "Love on a Porn Set: One Woman's Story," ABC News, www.abcnews.go.com/Primetime/story?id=132369.

[12] Luke Ford, "Porn Stars Speak Out," LUKE IS BACK, October 5, 2007 (Web address withheld due to graphic content).

[13] Lubben, *Truth*, 6.

[14] Ford.

[15] Josephine Vivaldo, "Christian Ex-Porn Star's Message to Kacey Jordan," *The Christian Post*, March 16, 2011.

[16] Katharine Sarikakis and Zeenia Shaukat, "The Global Structures and Cultures of Pornography: The Global Brothel," Feminist Interventions in International Communication: Minding the Gap, Critical Media Studies: Institutions, Politics, and Culture (Rowman & Littlefield, October 8, 2007), 113–14.

[17] Amis.

[18] Robert Jensen, "A Cruel Edge: The Painful Truth about Today's Pornography and What Men Can Do about It," Robert Jensen School of Journalism University of Texas, Austin. N.p., 2004, uts.cc.utexas.edu/~rjensen/freelance/pornography&cruelty.htm.

[19] Brian Gnatt, "Porn Star," *Michigan Daily* (Ann Arbor, MI) March 20, 1997, Weekend Magazine sec.: 3b.

[20] "Porn in the U.S.A.," 60 Minutes, CBS News, November 21, 2003, www.cbsnews.com/news/porn-in-the-usa-21-11-2003/.

[21] "Porn in the U.S. – here's a quiz," "American Porn," Frontline, PBS. www.pbs.org/wgbh/pages/frontline/shows/porn/etc/quiz.html, answer to question 10.

[22] Lubben, Truth, 3.

[23] Ford.

[24] Lubben, Truth, 3.

[25] Ibid., 2.

[26] Aly Weisman, "Here's What Female Porn Stars Get Paid for Different Types of Scenes," *Business Insider*, November 15, 2012, www.thedailybeast.com/articles/2013/11/23/the-adult-industry-doesn-t-pay-as-much-as-you-think.html/.

[27] Aurora Snow, "The Adult Industry Doesn't Pay! (As Much As You Think)," *The Daily Beast*, November 13, 2013, www.thedailybeast.com/articles/2013/11/23/the-adult-industry-doesn-t-pay-as-much-as-you-think.html.

[28] Paul M. Barrett, "The New Republic of Porn," "*Bloomberg Businessweek*," www.businessweek.com/articles/2012-06-21/the-new-republic-of-porn.

[29] Gene Ross, "The Porn Industry's Most Infamous Murders, Suicides, and Deaths," (Web address withheld due to graphic content).

[30] Adult Video News, "AVN's Top 50 Porn Stars of All Time," (Web address withheld due to graphic content).

[31] "Megan Leigh Porn Star," (Web address withheld due to graphic content).

[32] Dustin Siggins, "19-year-old college student commits suicide after shooting first porn scene," www.lifesitenews.com/news/19-year-old-college-student-commits-suicide-after-shooting-first-porn-scene.

[33] Lubben, Truth, 14–15.

[34] "Viagra ruining industry: porn stars," The Age, www.theage.com.au/articles/2002/07/05/1025667054825.html.

Chapter 9

[1] "Habit," *Merriam-Webster.*

Chapter 10

[1] "Accountability," Merriam-Webster.

[2] "Mandatory Reporters of Child Abuse and Neglect," www.childwelfare.gov/pubPDFs/manda.pdf.

Chapter 11

[1] David Kowalski, "Charles Spurgeon on Defending the Faith," ApologeticsIndex, 2013. www.apologeticsindex.org/3030-spurgeon-defending-the-faith.

[2] Devin Gordon, "John Wooden: First, How to Put on Your Socks," *Newsweek*, October 24, 1999, www.newsweek.com/john-wooden-first-how-put-your-socks-167942.

Chapter 12

[1] Slattery.

Chapter 14

[1] "The leadership survey on pastors and Internet pornography," *Leadership Journal*, January 1, 2001.

[2] *Apostolic Study Bible* (Hazelwood, MO: Word Aflame, 2014), 1024.

Chapter 15

[1] "Survey: Kids access porn sites at 6, start flirting online at 8," News10 abc. KXTV (Sacramento, California, 15 May 2013), Television.

[2] Ryan Dean, "Digital Safety," The Pentecostals of Bossier City (Bossier City, LA) April 8, 2015. Podcast.

[3] Nothstine.

[4] Cox Communications, "Teen Online & Wireless Safety Survey," May 2009, www.cox.com/wcm/en/aboutus/datasheet/take-charge/2009-teen-survey.pdf.

Chapter 16

[1] "The Leadership Survey on Pastors and Internet Pornography," *Leadership Journal, Christianity Today,* 2001, www.christianity-today.com/le/2001/winter/12.89.html.

Resources

Additional resources and information can be found on the Pure Morality Ministries website and Facebook page:

www.PureMorality.org

www.Facebook.com/PureMorality